MW01226693

~:~

How to Be Immortal

The Adventures of King Gilgamesh

and the

Wild Man

Steven A. Key

The NEW MUSE Book Series

Copyright © 2020 Steven A Key

Images provided by Shutterstock, Wikipedia Commons, and the Author.

The Books of the New Muse Series, by Steven A. Key, are a collection of writings focusing on the genres of Body, Mind & Spirit, neuroscience, psychology, consciousness, and ancient histories.

Ancient Shock ~ Monsters, Philosophers, & Saviors ~ How Neanderthals Became Sapiens ~ (2020)

How to Be Immortal ~ The Adventures of King Gilgamesh and the Wild Man ~ (2020)

The Vikings Secret Yoga ~ The Supreme Adventure (2019)

Future Books in the NEW MUSE Series

The Colors of Mind in the Garden of Knowledge

Psyche in the Theatre of the World

The Colors of Mind in Ancient Times: Egypt, India, Greece, China

The Death of Atheism and the Rise of the Spiritual Maverick

LIZ: Messages from Mother; The Connections beyond the Veil

Yeshua Esoterica: The Untold Story of Jesus

The Jungian Supernova: A Secret History of Psychiatry

Gotama's Take: The Rise and Fall of Mystical Buddhism

Dedication

This book is dedicated to the kindness, patience,

and heart-love of my Mother and to the strength,

discipline, and spirit-seed of my Father.

Hence, my Being.

These writings are also dedicated to those who lived long ago—
the ancient Sumer folk:

King Gilgamesh, Enkidu the Wildman, and Utnapishtim, the Immortal One

and also Stan Gooch, the world's first paleo-psychologist, who led the way
to understanding the psyche of the Neanderthal

Acknowledgements

First, I want to thank Baa'l Animingus as the one who assisted in the overall idea generation of this book and the New Muse Book Series. Turning an author's manuscript into modern book formats is somewhat of a miracle in itself. The creation of this book was facilitated by the many helpful, professional folks at BooksGoSocial, under the strong leadership of owner Laurence O'Bryan.

Literature is the faint remembrance of Experience.

Steven A. Key

Contents

Introduction

to

How to Be Immortal

The Adventures of King Gilgamesh and the Wild Man

'Gilgamesh is tremendous!'

Rainer Maria Rilke

The Long and Winding Road,
Which Leads Me to your Door.

The Beatles

When I first began writing about King Gilgamesh and the Wild Man, I was focusing on an amazing pattern of revelations that had occurred to me as I recently pored through the contents of the ancient Sumerian poem, many years after I had first encountered it in my youth.

The hoary Epic of Gilgamesh, which has puzzled many an academic scholar, is best seen, according to this author, not only as the world's oldest poem but also as the oldest written saga of Body, Mind & Spirit.

How to Be Immortal ~ The Adventures of King Gilgamesh and the Wild Man, is a remarkably different portrayal of the world's oldest poem, myth, or allegorical story, depending upon your view, of the 4,000-year-old Sumerian Epic. Most people, like myself, learned of King Gilgamesh and his adventurous exploits through their early school and university training, when they were forced to read nearly impossible interpretations, which usually contained extraordinarily little meaning. Thus, the Epic of Gilgamesh was rendered into a simple myth, which was little understood. In my own youth, I found the ancient poem rather boring . . . but what did I know? I was looking through an obscure lens, and simply following my academic training, just like everyone else. Now, however, many years later, we can reveal that the hoary Epic of Gilgamesh has really been, more than anything else, a true 'mystery of the millennia' to most scholars. Yet, there is more; much more.

In this dynamic portrayal, King Gilgamesh, and all of the Epic's major characters, are seen as living, breathing, embodied spiritual creatures. The great King of Sumer is actually the epitome of Body, Mind & Spirit, as are You. Perhaps that is the ancient author's great message, seen anew in this New Muse book.

> *"You are not a human being in search of a spiritual experience.*
>
> *You are a spiritual being immersed in a human experience.*
>
> *We are one, after all, you and I. Together we suffer,*
>
> *Together we exist, and forever will recreate each other."*
>
> **Pierre Teilhard de Chardin**

As in much ancient literature, the Epic of Gilgamesh has a well-received simple outer storyline, where the many famous exploits and journeys of a mythical, ancient Sumerian King are regaled, but more importantly, in *How to Be Immortal*, the powerful hidden story of another, far more spiritual Gilgamesh is, after 4,000 years, finally revealed.

In this book, a rough, yet sensitive, personal side to King Gilgamesh is observed. The Epic of Gilgamesh is portrayed as an inner saga of Body, Mind & Spirit, via the cuneiform carvings of a hoary, unknown, Mesopotamian scribe.

As exemplified by this ancient Sumerian poem, any individual, whether a King or an average person, male or female, progresses and journeys throughout their life; as they do, they encounter myriad, mysterious concepts embodied as ideas of Body, Mind & Spirit. The flowing of these three elements, into and out of each other, is likely the deepest science that a human can encounter. This electrical flowing of awareness could certainly be called Raja Yoga, with its great knowledge of connective processes, as described by Patanjali in his Yoga Sutras. In this book, we dig a bit deeper into the neural and electromagnetic aspects of our human, spiritual nature, while also describing an ancient ruler, who greatly puzzled, and anguished, over the specter of the harshness of life, death, and the thereafter. The elusive subject of God is fully contained in this tripartite expression of Body, Mind & Spirit. Even though we pull the mystic veil back here ever so slightly, it remains that nothing and no one can defeat Eternal Mystery and fully explain it. As we shall see, the entire process of 'explanation' is a human, left-brain phenomenon, and is extremely diminutive, when compared to a whole-brained mystical experience, which is the true, hidden, inside story of the Epic of Gilgamesh. As the King travels through the arduous adventures of his mortal life, he finally glimpses Immortality.

Come on You Raver, You Seer of Visions, Come on You Painter,

You Piper, You Prisoner, and Shine!

Pink Floyd

3

Portions of this book should be read slowly, as the Sumerian text is sometimes challenging, and also because of the numerous new, deep concepts for your consideration. As always, an open, curious mind is required when reading a New Muse Series book. Good reading to you.

Chapter 1 ~ The Great Neurological Divide of Body, Mind & Spirit

To Explain the Brains of Gilgamesh

Although it may seem unusual to the reader at first, before we begin our commentary on King Gilgamesh and the Wildman, a certain neuropsychological underpinning is necessary to explain specific key, repeated phrases in the Epic of Gilgamesh, concerning the 'makeup' or physical description of the King. These extremely cryptic phrases, which we identify in the next chapters, have much to do with a branch of neuroscience known as neuropsychological brain lateralism, or the study of the brain's frontal left and right hemispheres. Although the modern cognitive neurosciences generally do not attribute any neural knowledge to ancient peoples, we shall see that understanding the ancient King's brain configuration—his left and right hemispheres, and the rear brain as well—is an important key to understanding the Epic of Gilgamesh, which has baffled so many readers throughout the millennia, and appears especially confusing today.

The oldest poem in the world is thus often denigrated to the status of a children's myth, yet, in this New Muse book, we reveal incredible new hidden meanings.

In today's mainstream analytical neuroscience, there is an overly robotic left-brain approach to our marvelous and sacred human neural system, which we will call our Wisdom Body, in the manner of the ancient peoples.

The left-brain can be cold-hearted, controlling, and predatory, exactly like the young King Gilgamesh in the beginning of the Epic. Neuroscience now describes the 'entity' residing in this brain as the 'Self-Module', also commonly known as the Ego. Our Ego is a reductionist; it cognitively dissects everything it encounters, as it 'forms' its view of reality. While helpful in certain ways, this purely analytical method of left-brain functioning has severe shortcomings in that it does not address, nor acknowledge, the great hidden, whole being of our human neural nature. We gain our sentience, for example, by our ability to see things as being alive—a virtue imbued through our right hemisphere. If we spend our time simply analyzing the world, we will never see its life, beauty, and suffering.

Can't You See Its All Alive?

Seal

It's not enough to say, from a left-brain modality, that our cranium contains a brain that has, at last count, approximately 100 billion microscopic neural cells. The fantastic proportions of our interactive neural synaptic connections are placed at somewhere between 100 and 1000 *trillion* connections—numbers that are quite off the chart to imagine. Yet, hopefully, the astute reader will closely observe that thus far, we are merely talking about neuroscience statistical numbers. Yes, they are large, impressive numbers, but still . . . merely mapping the brain's componentry and 'counting and calculating' doesn't begin to approach the greatness of the human neurological system as an aspect of Body, Mind & Spirit. Not all scientists are mechanical thinkers, however. It is said that Einstein used to chalk up his blackboards at Princeton University with a few words of heady and humbling advice:

> *"Not everything that counts can be counted,*
>
> *and not everything that can be counted counts."*

Einstein was also adamant about moving beyond mere logical processes, that interpret the world as an endless series of lifeless objects:

> *"I believe in intuition and inspiration.*
>
> *Imagination is more important than knowledge.*
>
> *For knowledge is limited, whereas imagination embraces the*

6

entire world, stimulating progress, giving birth to evolution."

In a nutshell, we count and gain analytical knowledge with our left-brain hemisphere, and our intuition, inspiration, and imagination are fortunately supplied by our right brain, where the notions of sentiency, eternity, and timelessness are also found, as they were in the olden days of King Gilgamesh.

Also, we should note, purely analytical, mainstream neuroscience generally shuns or denigrates, the importance of the two brain hemispheres. As a result, there exists a small branch of underappreciated neuropsychologists, such as Oxford's Iain McGilChrist, who strongly advocate for an alternative, emotionally deeper approach to understanding the human neural system, in a whole-brained way. We are more than just a bunch of neurons busily making hay. As a leading brain lateralist, McGilChrist's understanding of a whole-brained approach to humanity and its culture, is decidedly more appealing as it explains the truer relations in our neural makeup.

Most people have heard and vaguely understand that they have two brain hemispheres—one on the left and one on the right—but the public lay knowledge generally stops there. Because the importance of the hemispheres is so crucial to knowing the ancient King of Sumer, we will now introduce Dr. Roger Wolcott Sperry, the winner of the 1981 Noble prize in neuroscience, who stunned the scientific community for a brief period with his discovery of the traits of the left and right brain hemispheres.

Sperry's Shock:

Extraordinary Evidence of Brain Lateralization

*"When the brain is whole, the **unified** consciousness of the left and right hemispheres add up to more than the individual properties of the separate hemispheres."*

Dr. Roger Wolcott Sperry

In the early days of neuroscience, experimental research found that severing the corpus callosum, the brain's critical neural 'wiring harness' which connects the left and right hemispheres, would immediately relieve the severe, life-threatening symptoms of spasmodic, epileptic patients. After their unique operation, the split-brain patients, as they came to be known, exhibited both normal and bizarre personality traits.

After studying these patients for years, Sperry's split-brain research created a new paradigm of sorts, but, like any great finding, the implications of brain lateralism, which localized important personality traits, both good and bad, into each brain region, was extremely hard for most analytical neuroscientists to absorb. Most importantly, Sperry wrote that over ninety percent of human beings are 'left-brain-dominant,' with the small remainder being more whole-brained; these few were creatively engaged so that the right hemisphere was also artfully utilized. Sperry's finding implies that the 'masses of humanity' are focused upon the dominant values that are now known traits belonging to our left brain. Having an overly materialistic focus in life, as did young Gilgamesh, is just one example of having a left-brain dominant lifestyle.

Now, remarkably, just a few years later, we find that the quintessential science of brain lateralism has been shoved aside and is now an often-ignored field in the analytical neurosciences. This neural ostracization of McGilChrist and Sperry, leaders in their field, is made by the same neural folks who originally informed us, as simple neural counters, that we only use 10% of our brain, a notion that is now quietly seen as being laughable and ridiculous. But, as we shall see, there is a marvelous hidden depth beyond the usual, customary neural descriptions of the brain hemispheres.

Our aspects of Body, Mind & Spirit, as well as our humanity—including the ancient King of Gilgamesh and Enkidu the Wildman—are not neatly summed up in a short, succinct list of neural features and traits. As they say, "The Map is not the Territory"; we are all living, breathing creatures, divinely infused, and making our way through life, as did King Gilgamesh. That is the deeper, spiritual message imbued in the ancient Epic of Sumer.

On the other end of the hemispheric spectrum, Dr. Iain McGilChrist, in his tome *The Master and his Emissary; The Divided Brain and the Making of the Western World* launches into a much deeper, and broader understanding of the cranial brains, which we will briefly discuss here, along with other neuroscience sources.

McGilChrist considers the 'Master' as the wiser but silent right-brain hemisphere; the right hemi-field which knows much but literally cannot 'speak.'
On the other hand, the 'Emissary' as the left-brain Ego presence which *can* speak, is portrayed as an unwilling, former servant of the wise, observing Master. McGilChrist's observations are identical to an ancient Chinese mystic's—surely this is no coincidence. Ancient peoples knew how to write about their personal, even neural attributes, in a highly accurate way.

> *"He who Speaks does not Know.*
>
> *He who Knows does not Speak."*
>
> **Tao Te Ching; Lao Tzu**

McGilChrist's idea of a powerful 'Emissary-Ego', like King Gilgamesh, is portrayed as a *runaway psychological force* that ultimately degrades or destroys the entire known world. The evolutionary development of our left-brain dominance may result in a degraded or even fatal end for our species.

This is actually predicted by ancient peoples in several cultures. The robotic insistence upon seeing reality, and people, as a machine-like conjecture, as something to be controlled, used, or consumed is a left-brain trait observed in French Philosopher Rene Descartes, the famous Logician and creator of the axiom, "I Think, Therefore I Am." Descartes wrote, in his strange *Meditations on First Philosophy*, that he would sit morbidly and look outside his window at the people passing by, dressed in their hats and coats. He was fascinated, but not because they were passing souls or human beings, but rather, because he, in his robot vision, saw the passersby as mechanical units, as walking machines, instead of living, breathing people.

Welcome my Son, to the Machine.

Pink Floyd

In his day, an uncaring cold-hearted King Gilgamesh treated the Sumer people in a similar way—as mere fodder; as animals for his base desires.

As Iain McGilChrist has suggested, severe left-brain dominance can be seen as a madness in its own right. An integrative philosopher, such as David Levin as quoted below, sees clearly through the subtle ruse of Descartes, who is dearly loved by those in the purely analytical neuroscientific community.

"What could be a greater symptom of madness than to look out of

one's window and see (what might for all one knows, be)

machines, instead of real people?"

Levin considers that mechanical-only thinkers, such as Descartes and other logicians of his time, are actually exhibiting a deep-set psychological paranoia, possibly as a result of a neural, hemispheric imbalance.

As we shall see, young King Gilgamesh, in his personal methods of severe dominance of his own people, can also be portrayed as an unbalanced, inwardly insecure ruler. In the Epic, the ancient poet reveals that the King has to grow psychologically if he wants to find his true inner nature, which is portrayed as partially human, and partially God-like, by the ancient Sumerian poet-scribe.

While the many fields in neuroscience can, of course, be rather deep and complex, we are only going to focus here on those aspects of neurophysiology and neuropsychology that help to explain the ancient view, as in the upcoming Body, Mind & Spirit example of King Gilgamesh.

The reader doesn't need a neuroscience degree or background to follow the ancient, intuitive reasoning that pertains to this ancient Sumerian ruler. There are only a few key points to be made here, as we describe the human Body, Mind & Spirit as a neural concert of sorts, marvelously operating either as a standalone Ego, or as a conscious Wisdom Body, where a greater aspect of conscious awareness is beginning to arise in the individual. This is the eternal consciousness that King Gilgamesh eventually seeks after his arduous journeys.

This new expansive awareness that grows in a person, whether ancient or modern, is usually filtered through the various vehicles of religious expression, where we see different flavorings and flowerings of humanity's sacred, neural nature.

So, what elements comprise this neural concert of our Wisdom Body, which we can hopefully know as our own self? Most layfolk vaguely understand that our cranium contains a brain, which has neurons to help us think, but their interest and knowledge generally stop there. The truth is that our skull actually contains several 'cooperating' brains, along with a subtle neural intelligence energetically coursing through our entire body, the salient points of which we will briefly discuss here before we engage the Saga of King Gilgamesh in the next chapter.

As humans slowly evolved over the eons, a remarkable neurodiversity unfolded. Neuroscience has now discovered neural intelligence, i.e. neuron cells in the heart, gut, and blood, and a clear-cut three-way brain system in our skulls. There is a tremendous amount of neural communication going on, yet analytical psychologists inform us that we are ninety-five percent unconscious. But we should ask: What of the Mystical Awareness, a subject of great importance in the Epic of Gilgamesh?

King Gilgamesh and Three-Brain Theory:

I n addition to the important brain-hemispheric research we have observed, there arose yet another key development relating to neurophysiology and neuropsychology.

In the 1960s, Dr. Paul MacLean, one of the brightest minds over at the National Institute for Health, was the first neuroscientist to note interesting neural evolutionary accretions in his original *Triune Brain Theory*. He specifically observed a type of 3-dimensional scaffolding, or layering, in our cranial brains. MacLean described the Triune brain as a Neo-Cortex, containing the topmost outer layers (which are divided into the left and right hemispheric brains) and the lower, deeper brain layers of the older Mammalian and Reptilian brains. The word *Triune* refers to the three layers of evolutionary tissue structures. Yes, dear reader, you are, ahem, part lizard; just don't tell your friends. Take a deep breath . . . and then realize that your deeper, rear lizard brain is actually running that show— meaning your very breath of life. This primordial rear brain is responsible for the core, essential requirements for your very being; moment to moment.

We recall that Yogis and other mystical folk seriously contemplate their own breathing for a very deep reason—that of a mystical spiritual union. Yet the primordial, inner brain—our neurally dense paleo-cerebral complex—remains largely a mystery to modern neuroscience. MacLean had another remarkable insight when he noted what he called the 'angel lobes,' referring to the top prefrontal cortex containing the two separated hemispheres. As we shall see, he may have been only half-right in this regard . . . because one of these angels can act much more like a demon, as the Ego which is housed in the left hemi-field.

Our right hemisphere, which houses our dreaming component, and our sense of timelessness and eternity, is definitely much more akin to the idea of an angel inside of ourselves. When, in the Epic of Gilgamesh, the King acts like a demon, or reveals his violent rage, he is portrayed as evil and ignorant, not unlike McGilChrist's portrayal of a runaway, egotistical leader in the world today, destroying everything in his path, as he goes along.

After understanding MacLean's notion of the Triune Brain, we can see additional wisdom in the insight of senior neurologist Marcel Kinsbourne, the director of the Oxford and New York Cognitive Neuroscience Laboratories. Kinsbourne maintains that the human cranium actually has three (3) sets of opponent processors, or contentious brain-sets; each contains mutually opposed elements whose contrary influences make possible finely calibrated responses to complex situations. Besides the left/right hemispheric arrangement, there is also the up/down neural pairing, where the effects of the overlying cortex inhibits or dampens the more basic automatic responses of the underlying subcortical regions. The third set of opposing brainworks—deemed the front/back tension—lies between the frontal lobes, which inhibit, or govern the rear posterior cortex in the rear of the skull.

Concerning a Cosmic Gilgamesh, we can ask a question: did ancient peoples, such as the scribes and poets of ancient Sumer, use different names and phrases to represent these neural 'governors,' that co-existed inside themselves?

Dr. MacLean's Triune Brain theory has also recently been the subject of interpretation by Buddhist scholars. Canadian author Suwanda H. J. Sugunasiri, in his newly published work, *Triune Mind, Triune Brain*, links MacLean's theory with the three-function model of the mind in Buddhism: Mano (receiving), Viññāna (executive) and Citta (judging). While MacLean labels the three evolved brains as Neomammalian, Paleomammalian, and Reptilian, Sugunasiri considers the consciousness attributes and activities of the three brains and renames them: Neosentient, Paleosentient, and Protosentient. Collectively he calls them the Triune Mind, which springs from the Triune Brain. Suwanda's Primary focus is on sentiency as a key feature in one's development of the Buddhist view. Sentiency is an attribute found in the right brain hemisphere.

14

Somehow, the ancient Sumerian scribe who wrote the ancient Epic knew of these marvels of the brain, and therefore described King Gilgamesh in the description of his total being as such.

The Tale of Two Birds

Before we get to King Gilgamesh, we should demonstrate an example of similar ancient literature, which also contains symbolic ideas that reflect neural distinctions, if not 'governorship,' as Kinsbourne described.

A remarkable intuitive piece of brain-hemispheric literature is subtly placed in the *Parable of Two Birds* which is embedded in both the Rig Veda and the Mandukya Upanishad, both older Hindu scriptures. The telltale hemispheric attributes we have been discussing are subtly expressed in the Indus prose. The Upanishad version is interpreted here, as Vedanta knowledge by Sri Aurobindo:

"Two birds, beautiful of wings, close companions, cling to one common tree: of the two, one eats the sweet fruit of the tree, the other eats not but watches his fellow. The soul is the bird that sits immersed on the common tree; but because he is not lord he is bewildered and has sorrow. But when he sees that other who is the Lord and the beloved, he knows that all is His greatness and his sorrow passes away from him. When, a seer, he sees the Golden-hued, the maker, the Lord, the Spirit who is the source of Brahman, then he becomes the knower and shakes from his wings sin and virtue; pure of all stain he reaches the supreme identity."

The theme of Sri Aurobindo's translation of the *Parable of the Two Birds* is not unlike that of McGilChrist's 'Master and the Emissary,' except that the modern state of the left-brain, runaway Ego-Emissary is nowhere near as sorrowful in the relenting of the soulful bird in the ancient parable. Indeed, the modern left-brain Ego is becoming more and more aggressive and relentless and demonstrates a growing lack of capacity for humility,

16

and hence the loss of spirituality. The clinically minded neuroscience community has assigned the left-brain entity a new moniker: The Self-Module. While the term Self-Module smacks of pure analytical, if not robotic thinking, there are more wholesome descriptions. Here is how Rabindranath Tagore (1861–1941), the influential Bengali polymath and artist-poet-playwright, interpreted the two-bird metaphor:

"In the Upanishads, it is said in a parable that there are two birds

sitting on the same bough, one of which feeds and the other looks on. This

is an image of mutual relationship of the infinite being and the finite self.

The delight of the bird which looks on is great, for it is pure and free

delight. There are both of these birds in man himself, the objective one

with its business of life, the subjective one with its disinterested joy of

vision."

Rabindranath seems to tell us that the act of seeing is more imaginative, more creative, more real than the act of practical knowing. The delight of the bird that looks on is greater than that of the bird that is busy with the facts of life. The left hemisphere, of course, is the practical 'just-the-facts' nature; the quiet, imaginative, creative nature is on the right side of our awareness—it can be our joy of vision.

Vision Flow

According to brain-lateralist neuroscience, there is a remarkable, yet little-known flow of vision processes, which illustrates the nature of our cranial brains.

When we view the outside world with our eyes, our optic process first delivers the perception or information to the visual cortex in the rear brain. Then something remarkable happens. Roughly speaking, the perception travels from the rear brain's visual cortex up to the right hemisphere, where the visual perception is seen in a Gestalt modality; the right-hemi-field sees 'everything at once'—this is its nature. The right hemisphere is pictorial as it sees whole images. Then, after two milliseconds or so, the incoming perception, now stored in the right hemisphere is sent to the left brain, arriving via a neural wiring harness called the corpus callosum.

What this means, is the perceiving Ego, or Self-Module, is at the tail-end of the vision process. One might refer to it as 'the last neural house on the left.' As the old saying goes, "the buck stops here," for the Ego is the last remaining vestige of consciousness in this ever-flowing divine process of awareness.

It is the Great Interpreter of Reality, but it has lost its way. This is also the story of our errant Sumerian King.

The Interpreter

The Thinker; Rodin

~!~

"The Unexamined Life is not worth Living"

Plato

In the early days of neuroscience, experimental research found that severing the corpus callosum, the brain's critical neural 'wiring harness' which connects the left and right hemispheres, would immediately relieve the severe, life-threatening symptoms of spasmodic, epileptic patients.

After studying these split-brain patients for years, neuropsychologist Michael S. Gazzaniga and neuroscientist Joseph E. LeDoux developed the neural hypothesis of the 'left-brain-interpreter.' It was also determined that *everyone* has this aspect of themselves, not just the split-brain patients.

Deeply understanding the left and right hemispheres and their connection to the rear brain from a sentient point of view as integrated living organisms interacting together, is an aspect of our neural being and our neural sentiency, often widely overlooked.

With the left hemi-field, we constantly interpret, explain, fathom, understand, or attempt to make sense of the tremendous, often overwhelming presentation coming to us from our deeper nature, our right hemisphere, and the densely packed rear brain. Every day, moment-by-moment, our incoming sensory world perceptions arrive slightly 'late' to the left-brain, which makes a tremendous attempt to construct a seemingly tangible reality from what might be considered random chaos by an analytical mind, of the Ego. But *why* does the information flow from the eyes to the rear brain's vision center and then up to the right hemisphere and not the left? The answer is remarkable, as it turns out—this is the *only* neural pathway.

It has recently been discovered that, although the two brain hemispheres look remarkably similar in appearance, there is a massive difference in the length of the 'arms' of the neuron cells themselves in each hemisphere. This difference may be one of the most telling factors in our human neural makeup. As we shall see, it even affects King Gilgamesh, as the ancient Sumer scribe coyly describes him as being both man . . . and God.

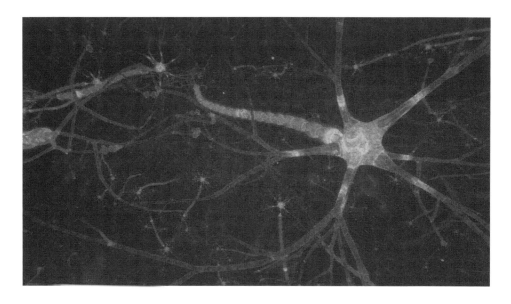

Image of axon arms extending away from the neuron nucleus.

Neurons communicate with each other via extensive networks of dendrites and axons, that serve as the vehicles for the all-important neural synapse network, which collectively produces trillions of neural transactions, as one hundred billion cranial neurons communicate with each other.

The left hemisphere has neurons with *extremely short* armlengths; the neural filaments cannot, and do not, reach down beyond the left brain into the older mammalian and reptilian brain-sets. On the other hand, the right hemisphere has neurons with *much longer* neural arms; these can and do reach several inches below into the older mammalian and reptilian brains. Thus, the vision path flows from the rear brain complex up to the front right hemisphere, simply because it can.

The dreamless and awake left-brain Ego, in this regard, seems orphaned from its own deeper connections. It relies upon its interpretive skills for its survival. Now, in this author's view, the longer length of the right hemisphere's connections down to the older rear-brain areas may be seen as **creating a neural 'entity'** by brain alignments. The Ego may choose from an endless variety of available spiritual names (the left hemisphere houses the naming function) to call this God.

A right hemisphere/rear-brain coordination is seen in both the vision flow we have discussed, and also in the dreaming capabilities of both brains. The left hemisphere does not dream. The right hemisphere is responsible for seeing the world as alive, and sentient in all ways; it is only the left hemi-field that is predatory and considers life merely as objects to be controlled.

Somehow, the ancient scribes of Sumer intuitively knew of this energetic, neural situation, and personified them in an evil young King, who was greatly changed by love and death, into a spiritual Seeker.

"Lo, he that cometh to us—'tis the flesh of the gods is his body."

The Epic of Gilgamesh

Gilgamesh: One-Third Man, Two-Thirds God

Scholars have puzzled for centuries over a pressing question. In the 4,000-year-old Epic, how is it that King Gilgamesh was referred to as *one-third Man and two-thirds God*, in the ancient times of Sumer?

At first blush a daunting question, but one we can solve with a clearer definition of what is being hinted at by the scribe of the Epic.

Let us consider that such an unusual reference is actually a neuro-spiritual description. We are not so far off from Chardin's words of being a 'spiritual creature having a human experience' if we add a few neural details and examples to help complete the puzzle.

The Epic of Gilgamesh, with its great age, is the first human literature to depict a human creature as a God-like being too. Our premise that this ancient notion has decidedly neural implications is strengthened by using subsequent cultural examples which also have used similar neural depictions. The neural depiction is always couched in implicit poetic, or spiritual words, as seen below in the examples of the Norse Odin, and the Hindu Nara-Narayana.

Nara-Narayana

In the Hindu literature, there are several interesting references to our cranial 'neural governors' that infer ancient, spiritual knowledge of how the brain hemispheres can interact. This interaction can be seen in the names, traits, and functions of the people and deities in the numerous legends and allegorical myths. In particular, the story of Nara-Narayana comes to mind. In one sense, they are collectively referred to as *The Sages of Nara-Narayana*. Nara is the human aspect, extended into the outer world at large. Narayana is the divine aspect, representing the vast inner nature. Together, these two entities are symbolically housed in the neural body of humankind.

Nara-Narayana is a Hindu deity pair. Nara-Narayana is the twin-brother

avatar of the God Vishnu on earth, working for the preservation of

dharma or righteousness. In the concept of Nara-Narayana, the human

soul Nara is the eternal companion of the Divine Narayana.

Nara-Narayana, Wikipedia

We can further consider that Nara is the naïve Ego, or the blossoming Soul, depending upon its development. Nara represents the personal side of humankind, largely housed in the left hemisphere. It could be said that it is the Nara that names and writes the entire legend of Nara-Narayana, while the Narayana is silent on the matter.

Together, they can be considered as a higher and lower 'deity pairing.'

One legend states that the Hindu God Vishnu descends into the Narayana avatar; this poetic language represents the right hemisphere with its capacity for timelessness and the sense of endless being. When Narayana 'delivers' its messages and presence to Nara across the corpus callosum, it is important to note that Nara, our human Ego, operating as the left-hemispheric interpreter, will always color, or influence, the divine transmission according to its filters of culture and upbringing, and even the karma of the Nara. Nara, as the left brain, always creates its daily view of life, its worldview. Conversely, in an unawakened state, the Nara mentally occludes its karma, that hidden knowledge of past lives, and also, the great awareness of the Narayana, which we may refer to as the transcendental Wisdom Body.

We could substitute many different naming conventions in a number of different cultures to reflect this simple, ancient observation of how our left-brain consciousness and right-brain deep awareness actually work. Although couched in poetic imagery, the underlying function of cranial interactions can still be seen as a singular integrated process.

24

A mature state of Nara-Narayana describes a psychological, integrated 'Fluid Identity' of strongly flowing consciousness and awareness, moving through the localized mind of the Ego, the Nara, and the infinity offered by the Narayana.

The principles of Nara-Narayana are intrinsic to humankind, although appearing under always-differing names. This is why Joseph Campbell noted that ancient cultures often behaved syncretically; they recognized the Gods of other cultures as having similar functions, but different names, and so he noted that great conquerors such as the Romans, were tolerant in their treatment of spiritual practices of other cultures, so long as they did not resist the imposed governing state.

The legend of Nara-Narayana is found in several instances in Hindi literature. The epic Mahabharata identifies the God Krishna (an avatar of Vishnu) with Narayana and Arjuna, the chief hero of the epic, as the human Nara.

In disregarding the names for the moment and focusing on function, we again see a God is talking to a human; this is the ancient belief system that is so ubiquitous in many cultures. In each case, we can represent the human as the extended personality of the egoic self, and the vast, limitless, unspoken potential of the right hemisphere, coupled with the primordial rear brain, as the deity that is sensed and approached—even surrendered to.

It's important to recall that the right hemi-field has neurons that have greatly extended axon 'arms' that can reach deeply into non-contiguous tissues, such as the emotive limbic and primordial rear brain areas. Because of this 'extra reach,' the abilities and communications of the right hemisphere are greatly extended. The left hemi-field, in contrast, while seeming to be nearly identical to the right side, does not have neurons with extended arms, thus, it is largely confined to its own neural tissue, and doesn't reach into the depths of older neural areas, which are the most neurally dense and primordial. Thus, Nara, by itself, is largely an orphan in a very strange universe. However, once Narayana is realized, then the universal doors open, always painted with the filters of our own neural making. Another interpretation of the word Narayana renders Nara as meaning "human" and Ayana as "direction/goal." In this sense, Nara-Narayana refers to the proper "direction of a human" as finding shelter or liberation in the divine side; Narayana, which is an inner, neural direction that all potentially whole-brained people can follow. How far can this direction go? Endlessness is a feature of our right hemisphere.

In continuing the focus on integrated neural processes that produce both distinct personal consciousness and religious culture, one could say that the cranial Nara-Narayana is the **avatar** for the transcendent, energy-intelligent Heart, with its own pulsing neural center.

In many Hindu spiritual systems, as in the case of Shiva, a spiritual retreat into the Heart is seen as the transcendent goal; some may even say the true source of Narayana, who is also called Para-Braham.

All of these names, traits, and ideas, deal with the nature of the sentient, integrated neural system—our inherent human nature, with its implied, largely unseen Divinity. There are other notable examples of neuro-spiritual Hindu literature. In later chapters, we shine a new light on the neural nature of the AUM itself, as stated in the ancient Hindu Devanagari script, and the Upanishads.

Odin's Eye, the Ego, and the Wisdom Body

The curious 10th century Viking saga of how Odin, the chief deity, lost his eye, can be seen as another interesting allegory with neuropsychological implications. Below is an excerpt taken from a New Muse Book, *The Vikings Secret Yoga ~ The Supreme Adventure*:

"As seen from inside the skull, the right eye is owned and operated by the brain's left hemisphere, while the left eye is associated with the right brain. As we recall, modern neuroscience now states that the "self-module," as our personalized Ego, is largely residing in the left brain.

In the various scenes presented in the Vikings Poetic Edda, the clever trick of the Norse bards is in symbolically encrypting the Yogic need of reducing, or controlling, the negativity of the Ego. They cleverly said that

26

Odin needed to sacrifice his right eye, if the God wanted to obtain true wisdom.

Thus, when Odin's right eye is plucked out, the psychological impasse caused by the dominating Ego is eliminated, and the great wisdom of the deeper, dreamlike right hemisphere and primordial rear brain, begins to flow into the consciousness of the individual. Odin became enlightened and wise, in this ancient portrayal of Ego-sacrifice. The Celts, a thousand years before the Vikings, also had Gods who sacrificed their eye in a similar fashion.

After a bit of deciphering, we find the Vikings and Celts used quite simple but telling poetic and symbolic language; if you truly eliminate the eye of your Ego, all will be revealed.

Neuroscience, according to neuropsychologist Dr. Karl Pribram, fully recognizes that the right hemisphere can "see everything at once," as in a Gestalt modality; however, this process is severely limited by the inhibitions put in place by the left hemisphere, which prefers to see through its own interpretive view, leading to an analyzed and substantially reduced picture of reality."

Aldous Huxley once referred to this limited conscious state as being a mere "trickle of reality." By giving up the eye of his Ego, the remaining left eye of the right hemisphere shines forth: Odin became known as wise and all-seeing. As we shall see, in order for King Gilgamesh to become wise, he too will sacrifice his one-third humanness . . . to the greater two-thirds of his divine being. The Saga Remains the Same.

Chapter 2 ~ The Ancient Tablets

T
he Epic of Gilgamesh, that marvelous poem of ancient Mesopotamia, is regarded as the earliest surviving great work of literature.

Archaeologists Hormazd Rassam and Sir Austen Henry Layard discovered thousands of partially broken tablets in the mid-nineteenth century, previously lost to the world for thousands of years, lying in the ancient Sumerian cities of Nimrud and Nineveh. A small portion of these cuneiform writings centered on spiritual hymns and poems. Twelve of these hoary tablets would eventually be deciphered by England's George Smith, who soon declared that these specific tablets revealed the ancient Epic of Gilgamesh. Smith and other scholars pored over the ancient cuneiform writings and found several amazing concepts scratched upon the clay tablets. The first known depiction of a great, devastating flood was found in the Epic of Gilgamesh. Scholars have since confirmed that this Mesopotamian literary 'event' was later found copied into a somewhat plagiarized Bible, becoming the Christian story of Noah and his Ark, along with many other ancient borrowed stories.

Like the ancient flood, the 'Wisdom Body' of Gilgamesh is another such legend. He is one-third Man and two-thirds God. While many versions of the Epic poem have since been found with Babylonian, Akkadian, and Sumerian accents, it is generally agreed that the epic poem was first written in 2100 BCE in ancient Sumer. Today, however, researchers must consider the Epic of Gilgamesh as a chronological series of slightly adapted tales, which may be viewed as a patchwork quilt of enhanced cultural ideas. Whilst occasionally cited, this ancient book is almost never seen today as it is extremely rare, even in libraries. This is due to it being long out of print (in fact, it has never been reprinted). We will be using quotations taken from the baseline translation of Gilgamesh, by Oxford's R. Campbell Thompson, in 1928. Thompson created the following descriptions, seen here by tablet:

The First Tablet: Of the Tyranny of Gilgamesh; the Creation of Enkidu

The Second Tablet: Of the Meeting of Gilgamesh and Enkidu

The Third Tablet: Expedition to the Forest of Cedars against Huwawa

The Fourth Tablet: The Arrival at the Gate of the Forest

The Fifth Tablet: Of the Fight with Huwawa

The Sixth Tablet: Of the Goddess Ishtar, Who Fell In Love With the Hero After His Exploit Against Huwawa

The Seventh Tablet: The Death of Enkidu

The Eighth Tablet: Of the Mourning of Gilgamesh, and What Came of It

The Ninth Tablet: Gilgamesh In Terror of Death Seeks Eternal Life

The Tenth Tablet: How Gilgamesh Reached Uta-Napishtim

The Eleventh Tablet: The Great Flood

The Twelfth Tablet: Gilgamesh, In Despair, Enquires of the Dead

In this book, we do not rigidly cover the details of each story outlined in each tablet. An example is the Sixth tablet, concerning the goddess Ishtar and her wooing of Gilgamesh; this tablet is not essential or necessary to our theme. Our focus is upon the spirituality of King Gilgamesh, Enkidu, and the mysterious Uta-Napishtim—the Immortal One.

Chapter 3 ~ Enter Enkidu The Wildman

Tablet I

Of the Tyranny of Gilgamesh, and the Creation of Enkidu.

M ost Sumerian scholars focus on the first part of the Epic, with its colorful outer storyline of young King Gilgamesh and his encounter with wild Enkidu. During his early days, Gilgamesh was an abomination; he certainly didn't act or seem to be one-third Man and two-thirds God. The arrogant, cruel King raped young betrothed girls and enslaved the young men of the city. The oppressed people of Uruk had thus cried out to the Gods (Moon God, Hear my Plea!) and mysteriously, shortly thereafter, an extremely strong, primitive, red-furred wild man named Enkidu appeared, as if sent from the Gods to challenge the King, for the evil treatment of his own people.

"Gilgamesh leaveth no son to his father,

his arrogance swelling each day and night.

Gilgamesh leaveth no maid to her mother,

nor daughter to hero, Nay, nor a spouse to a

husband. And so, to the appeal of their wailing

Gave ear the Immortals"

The Epic's outer plot begins with a Sumerian hunter on the outskirts of the city of Uruk who finds that someone has been destroying his traps. Enkidu, it seems, has been setting the trapped animals free, thinking they are his kin. The hunter spies Enkidu in the woods and later informs King Gilgamesh of the intrusion by this strange creature, matted with red hair, who exhibits such great strength as to rival the powerful King himself.

"Sprouted luxuriant growth of his hair-like, the awns of the barley,

Nor knew he people nor land; E'en with gazelles did he pasture on

herbage, along with the cattle drank he his fill, with the beasts did his heart delight at the water."

"Then did a hunter, a trapper, come face to face with this fellow, came

on him one, two, three days, at the place where the beasts drank their

water Sooth, when the hunter espied him, his face o'er mantled with

terror."

~!~

There is no mention in the Epic concerning the parents of Enkidu, just the inference that he was a God-sent individual. This author considers that, setting the Fates aside in the Epic, Enkidu represents a hybrid-hominid type of creature, a Neanderthal-Sapiens mix, and is not fully human, as compared to King Gilgamesh. More information on this unusual subject is available in an upcoming New Muse Book, *Ancient Shock ~ Monsters, Philosophers, & Saviors ~ How Neanderthals Became Sapiens* (Fall 2020). Enkidu is not treated as a mythical creature in the New Muse Series, but something much more . . . a true Wildman of the past, whose parents will remain forever unknown. He was an only child, alone and wild.

And my dear Mother left me . . . when I was quite young.

On the Road Again; **Canned Heat**

Enkidu is not normal; he is described as a strange wild man. At first, Enkidu lives in the wild plain amongst animals, and knows nothing of human life.

The hunter returns to the gates of Uruk, immediately seeks out King Gilgamesh in his court and excitedly informs him of the strange encounter. He calls him 'father,' as a sign of royal respect.

Open'd his mouth, the hunter, and spake, addressing his father:

"Father, there is a great fellow come forth from out of the mountains,

O, but his strength is the greatest the length and breadth of the country.

His strength is enormous! Ever he rangeth at large o'er the mountains,

and ever with cattle. Grazeth on herbage and ever he setteth his foot to

the water, so that I fear to approach him. The pits which I myself

hollow'd with mine own hands hath he fill'd in again, and the traps of

my setting torn up, and out of my clutches hath escape all the cattle.

Beasts of the desert: to work at my fieldcraft, he will not allow me."

~!~

There's danger on the edge of town.
The End; **The Doors**

The young King (the city father) listened intently to the trapper, and then responded firmly, speaking of his own great strength, and how to trap the red-haired Wildman, with the lure of a beautiful woman.

Open'd his mouth then his father, and spake, addressing the hunter

*"Gilgamesh dwelleth in Erech, my son, whom **no one** hath vanquish'd,*

Nay, but 'tis his strength is greatest, over the length and breadth of the country.

Go, O hunter, a courtesan-girl(a hetaera), take with thee.

When he the cattle shall gather again to the place of drinking,

So, shall she put off her mantle; the charm of her beauty revealing.

Then shall he spy her, and sooth, will embrace her.

~!~

And so the prostitute and the hunter went forth, to tenderly 'ambush' the young Enkidu, who grazed with the gazelles. When Enkidu the Wild Man appeared, the temple courtesan liked what she saw! The ancient trapper then tells her to seduce him, without delay.

~!~

Forth went the hunter, took with him a courtesan-girl, a hetaera.

So, did they start on their travels, went forth on their journey together,

Aye, at the term of three days arrived at the pleasance appointed.

*Sate they down in their **ambush,** the hunter and the hetaera,*

One day, two days they sat by the place where the beasts drank their

water. Then at last came the cattle to take their fill in their drinking.

Thither the animals came that their hearts might delight in the water,

Aye, there was Enkidu also, he whom the mountains had gender'd,

33

E'en with gazelles did he pasture on herbage, along with the cattle.

Drank he his fill with the beasts did his heart delight at the water.

So, beheld him the courtesan-girl, the lusty great fellow,

O but a monster, all savage, from out of the depths of the desert!

"'Tis he, O girl! O, discover thy beauty, thy comeliness shew him,

So that thy loveliness he may possess—(O), in no wise be bashful,

Ravish the soul of him, as soon as his eye on thee falleth,

He, forsooth, will approach thee, and thou—O, loosen thy mantle,

So that he clasp thee, and then with the wiles of a woman shalt ply him.

wherefore) his animals, bred in his desert, will (straightway) deny him,

since to his breast he hath held thee."

*The girl, displaying her bosom, shew'd him her comeliness, yea so that
he of her beauty possess'd him. Bashful she was not, but ravish'd the
soul of him, loosing her mantle, So that he clasp'd her, and then with the
wiles of a woman she plied him, holding her unto his breast. 'Twas thus
that Enkidu dallied.*

Tablet II; The King Meets the Wildman

To placate the distressed hunter, a Sumerian temple seductress—a sacred prostitute—is sent at the behest of King Gilgamesh to lure and distract the Wildman. She slowly coaxes Enkidu into moving towards human habitation near the ancient city of Uruk. While she is seducing him on the outskirts of Uruk, the woman also teaches him to speak, perhaps, we may consider, in both sign language as well as the mono-syllabic Sumerian language. With a combination of gestures and simple words, Enkidu, the red-furred Wildman, quickly comprehends and learns to understand her, and soon begins to speak.

Girl, you gotta love your man, make him understand.

Riders on the Storm; **The Doors**

"Thus, for six days, seven nights, with the courtesan-girl in his mating.

Broke into speech then, the nymph, and thus unto Enkidu spake she:

"Yea, as I view thee, e'en like a god, O Enkidu, shalt be,

Why with the beasts of the field dost thou ever range over the desert?

Up, for I'll lead thee to Erech (Uruk) broad-marketed, aye, to the Temple

Sacred, the dwelling of Anu—O Enkidu, come, that I guide thee,

Unto E-Anna, the dwelling of Anu, where Gilgamesh liveth."

Wild Enkidu, who runs and feeds with the gazelles, begins to understand human communication and the new ideas of civilization. When his new female companion tells him of the terrorized people of Uruk, and of the distasteful actions of the young ruler of Uruk, Enkidu senses the evil of the situation, and quickly makes up his mind to go and challenge the evil young King. Neither King nor Wildman has ever been defeated in battle.

~!~

Now, it appears our ancient Sumerian poet-scribe has an insight into Jungian dream-analysis, as he, or she, writes in the Epic, that, before Enkidu arrives in the city, Gilgamesh has two powerful, psychic dreams, possibly related, psychologically, to the strong message he received from the hunter, who was incredibly terrified when he first observed Enkidu in the wild. Later, Gilgamesh relates his dream to his mother, who is also a Sumerian goddess. His mother, in talking below, refers to Anu, a powerful Sumerian deity:

"Gilgamesh coming, spake to his mother, the dream to reveal.

'O my mother, a vision which I beheld in my night-time. Behold, there

were stars of the heavens, when something like unto Anu's own self

fell down on my shoulders, Ah, though I heaved him, he was o'er strong for

me, and though his grapple loosed I, I was unable to shake him from off

me. And now, all the meanwhile, people from Erech(Uruk) were standing

about him; the artisans pressing on him behind, while throng'ed him the

Hero's, my very companions, kissing his feet."

Then I presented him low at thy feet, that as mine own equal.

Thou might'st account him.'

She who knoweth all wisdom, to Gilgamesh thus did she answer:

'Lo, by the stars of the heavens are represented thy comrades,

36

That which was like unto Anu's own self, which fell on thy shoulders,

Which thou didst heave, but he was, o'erstrong for thee, aye, though

his grapple Thou didst unloose, but to shake him from off thee thou wert

unable, So, didst present him low at my feet, that as thine own equal

This is a stout heart, a friend, one ready to stand by a comrade,

One whose strength is the greatest, the length and breadth of the country.

Like to a double of Anu's own self his strength is enormous.

This is a sign that thou art the one he will never abandon:

This of thy dream is the meaning.'

Again he spake to his mother,

'Mother, a second dream did I see: Into Erech, the high-wall'd,

Hurtled an axe, and they gather'd about it: the meanwhile, from Erech

People were standing about it, the people all thronging before it,

Artisans pressing behind it, while I at thy feet did present it,

As mine own equal.'

She the all-wise, who knoweth all wisdom, thus answer'd her offspring,

'Lo, that Axe thou didst see is a Man; as thine own equal I might account

him. This is a stout heart, a friend, one ready to stand by a comrade,

37

One whose strength is the greatest the length and breadth of the country.

Like to a double of Anu's own self, his strength is enormous.'

Gilgamesh open'd his mouth, and addressing his mother, thus spake he:

'Though great danger befall, a friend shall I have . . .'"

~!~

The two dreams of King Gilgamesh were prescient indeed, but it was too early to call Enkidu a great friend, rather, he was the King's Adversary. Like Gilgamesh, Enkidu is also said to have been made from the clay of the Earth. When Enkidu enters Uruk to stop the raping by the arrogant young King, the people of the city gather to greatly admire the Wildman:

"As he stopp'd in the street of broad-marketed Erech, the people

thronging, behind him exclaim'd "Of a truth, like to Gilgamesh is he,

Shorter in stature a trifle, his composition is stronger. Once like a

weakling baby he suck'd the milk of the wild things! He, a mere savage

becometh a hero of proper appearance, Now, unto Gilgamesh, god-like,

his composition is equal."

As Enkidu enters Uruk to deter Gilgamesh from his evil actions, the Wildman blocks the doorway to the wedding house. Thus, Gilgamesh cannot come, as he is accustomed, to rape the betrothed on this special day.

The lustful King encounters the great red-bodied Enkidu standing in his way; Gilgamesh's recent dreams are forgotten, as he is enraged. The two fierce foes immediately fall to grappling and battle mightily, yet they are evenly matched as both have tremendous physical strength.

"Strewn is the couch for the love-rites and Gilgamesh, now in the night-time cometh to sleep, to delight in the woman, but Enkidu, coming there in the highway, doth block up the passage to Gilgamesh threat'ning He with his strength. Gilgamesh, behind him...burgeon'ed his rage and rushed to attack him; they met in the highway. Enkidu barr'ed up the door with his foot and to Gilgamesh entry would not concede. They grappled and snorted like bulls and the threshold shattered, the very wall quivered as Gilgamesh and Enkidu fought."

Friendship

Chapter 4 ~ The Birth and Death of Friendship

Life is a series of Hellos and Goodbyes.

And you find that the friends you had are gone forever.

Billy Joel

After their violent encounter, and as sometimes happens in life, the red-furred Enkidu and Gilgamesh soon became highly regarded peers and the best of friends. After their combat, and close to exhaustion, the two combatants cease their fierce struggle; the fight is a stalemate. Then, likely panting heavily from their efforts, the King and the Wild Man finally relent in their hostility and express mutual admiration for each other. A new and very unusual friendship is born, which was foretold by the King's earlier dreams.

40

"Gilgamesh bent his leg to the ground: so, his fury abated,

Aye, and his ardour was quell'd: so soon as was quelled his ardour,

Enkidu thus unto Gilgamesh spake: "Of a truth, did thy mother

bear thee as one, and one only"

So, when great warriors meet their match, there is great respect generated for the other fellow. The King matures quickly after the red-haired Wild Man admonishes him, and the horrible ruler immediately ceases his terrible actions of slavery and rape against the people of Uruk. The King tries and succeeds in mending his terrible behavior towards his own people. Afterwards, at the King's relentless behest, the two great fighters set out upon several kingly adventures; Gilgamesh is still very egotistical, and eager to prove his greatness by kingly feats.

During their ensuring travels, Enkidu and Gilgamesh arrive in the ancient Lebanon Forest of Cedars and meet and needlessly kill a hairy monster called Huwawa, as one example, of a young King's Ego. The King addresses the Enkidu the Wildman, in the next tablet.

Tablet III: Journey to the Cedar Forest and the Battle of Huwawa

Gilgamesh open'd his mouth, and to Enkidu spake he (in this wise):

"I, O my friend, am determined to go to the Forest of Cedars,

Aye and Huwawa the Fierce will o'ercome and destroy what is evil.

Then will I cut down the Cedar."

Enkidu open'd his mouth, and to Gilgamesh spake he (in this wise),

"Know, then, my friend, what time I was roaming with kin in the

mountains; I for a distance of two hours' march from the skirts of the

Forest into its depths would go down. Huwawa—his roar was a

whirlwind, Flame in his jaws, and his very breath Death! O, why hast

desired This to accomplish? To meet with Huwawa were conflict

unequall'd."

Gilgamesh open'd his mouth and to Enkidu spake he (in this wise):

"Tis that I need the rich yield of its mountains I go to the Forest"

~!~

Enkidu repeats his concern about encountering the great Huwawa, however, King Gilgamesh, in seeking great fame, is unperturbed, and attempts to persuade the fearful Enkidu to see his point of view:

"Gilgamesh open'd his mouth and to Enkidu spake he, in this wise:

"Who, O my friend, is unconquer'd by death? A divinity, certes,

Liveth for aye in the daylight, but mortals—their days are all number'd,

All that they do is but wind—But to thee, now death thou art dreading,

Proffereth nothing of substance thy courage, I, I'll be thy ward!

'Tis thine own mouth shall tell thou didst fear the onslaught of battle,

I, forsooth, if I should fall, my name will have stablish'd forever.

Gilgamesh 'twas, who fought with Huwawa, the Fierce!

In the future, after my children are born to my house, and climb up thee,

saying: 'Tell to us all that thou knowest'. Yea, when thou speakest, in

this wise, thou grievest my heart for the Cedar I am determined to fell,

that I may gain fame everlasting."

And so, after regaling Enkidu with tales of his future children, the King instructs his smith-forgers to fashion new weapons, for use when Gilgamesh, Enkidu, and fifty of the Sumer men travel to the ancient cedar forest. Once there they will cut down the finest trees and bring them back to Uruk, where they will construct a massive gate to the city.

However, Enkidu is beginning to show signs of a strange sickness; we may interpret this as a developing sexual disease, such as the debilitating syphilis, likely transmitted by the temple prostitute.

Tablet IV; The Arrival at the Gate of the Forest

Enkidu is stricken with fear at thought of the combat. Enkidu lay for a day, yea, a second, for Enkidu lying prone on his couch, was a third and

a fourth day...a fifth, sixth and seventh, eighth, ninth, and tenth. While

Enkidu lay in his sickness, th' eleventh, aye, till the twelfth, on his couch

was Enkidu lying. Call'd he to Gilgamesh, "O but, my comrade, hateth

me, because within Erech, I was afraid of the combat. Enkidu open'd his

mouth and spake unto Gilgamesh, saying: "Nay, but, my friend, let us no

wise go down to the depths of the Forest, For 'tis my hands have grown

weak, and my arms are stricken with palsy." Gilgamesh open'd his mouth

and spake unto Enkidu, saying: "Shall we, O friend, play the coward?

Thou shalt surpass them all. Thou, O my friend, art cunning in warfare,

art shrewd in the battle, So shalt thou of death, have no terror,

So that the palsy (now striking) thine arms may depart, and the weakness

pass from thy hands! Be brave and resist! O my comrade, together

We will go down—let the combat in no wise diminish thy courage!

O forget death, and be fearful of nothing, for he who is valiant.

Cautious and careful, by leading the way hath his own body guarded,

He 'tis will safeguard a comrade. A name by their valour they will

establish. And now they together arrive at the barrier, still'd into silence their speech, and they themselves (suddenly) stopping.

~!~

Tablet V; The Fight with Huwawa

The Epic continues with our travelers arriving at the edge of the beautiful ancient forest—dark, pristine and primordial, and strong smelling of cedar:

Stood they and stared at the Forest, they gazed at the height of the

Cedars, scanning the avenue into the Forest. And there where Huwawa

stalk'd, was a path, and straight were his tracks, and good was the

passage. They beheld the Mount of the Cedar, the home of th' Immortals,

shrine; the Cedar uplifting its pride 'gainst the mountain,

Fair was its shade, all full of delight, with bushes here spreading,

Spread, too, was the Cedar, with its incense.

~!~

Our two heroes and the King's men camp outside the aromatic forest for the night . . . and the King dreams once more. In the morning, Enkidu proves himself worthy of the Jungian analysis of symbols in dreams, as the two discuss yet another dream of Gilgamesh's:

"Then came another dream to me, comrade, and this second vision

was pleasant indeed, which I saw, for we twain were standing together,

high on a peak of the mountains, and then did the mountain peak topple,

Enkidu spake to his comrade the dream to interpret, thus saying:

"Comrade, in sooth, this vision, of thine unto us, good fortune forbodeth,

Aye, 'tis a dream of great gain thou didst see, for, bethink you, O

comrade, surely the mountain which thou hast beholden must needs be

Huwawa. Thus, doth it mean we shall capture Huwawa, and throw

down his carcass, leaving his corpse in abasement—to-morrow's

outcome will I shew thee".

In the early morning, the small group of Sumerian men, along with Enkidu, break camp and cautiously enter the cedar forest and travel for miles. During a rest, Gilgamesh prays to the great, looming mountains to grant him yet another prophetic dream. The mountain responds with a chill wind, and the King later dreams as he sleeps, and suddenly awakes with a start, and questions Enkidu:

~

Granted the mountain a dream; and it breathed on him.

Then a chill windblast up-sprang and a gust passing over

Made him to cower, and there he sway'd, like the corn of the mountains.

Gilgamesh, squatting bent-kneed, supported his haunches, and

straightway sleep, such as, floweth on man, and descended upon him at

midnight. Ending his slumber (all sudden), he hied him to speak to his

46

comrade: "Didst thou not call me, O friend? (O), why am I waken'd

(from slumber)? Didst thou not touch me—(for), why am I fearful(?), (or)

hath not some spirit Pass'd (me)? (Or,) why is my flesh (all) a-quiver?

~!~

The King then relates a violent dream, akin to that of an erupting volcano, which symbolically represents Huwawa, who will die.

A third dream, O comrade,

I have beheld: but all awesome this dream which I have beholden:

Loud did the firmament roar, and earth with the echo resounded,

Sombre the day, with darkness uprising, and lightning bolts flashing,

kindled were flames, and there, too, was Pestilence , fill'd to o'erflowing,

Gorgéd was Death! Then faded the glare, then faded the fires,

Falling, the brands turn'd to ashes.

~

After waking from his fiery dream, the King prays to Shamash the Sun for assistance in fighting the monstrous Huwawa; soon, a vicious battle ensues. Although the Epic's prose is terse here, we may imagine that a strong King, Enkidu, and dozens of Sumerian men encountered and then quickly surrounded the wild Huwawa, who, being greatly outnumbered, roared mightily at them, but to no avail. Powerful winds suddenly kicked up, mightily swaying the tall cedars to and fro. With no path of escape, the King of the Cedar Forest finally surrendered,

Unto th' entreaty of Gilgamesh hearken'd the Sun-god in heaven,

Wherefore against Huwawa he raised mighty winds: yea, a great wind,

Wind from the North, (aye), a wind from the South, yea a tempest and

storm wind, chill wind, and whirlwind, a wind of all evil: 'twas eight

winds he raised, Seizing Huwawa before and behind, so that nor to go

forwards, nor to go back was he able: and then Huwawa surrender'd.

The captured Huwawa, now roped and bound, pleads for his life—his large eyes evidently begging, and a short stuttering language consisting of a few vowel sounds seems to say *'Don't kill me.'* This is the creature's message to the victorious Gilgamesh. However, Enkidu tells the King in no uncertain terms that Huwawa must die, or he may one day seek revenge and turn against the King. And so, the King of Sumer turns quickly and cuts off the head of the great, hairy Huwawa; the protector of the forest. The Men of Uruk then proceeded to cut down the finest cedar timbers, to be shaped unto a new gate for the city of Uruk.

(Author's note: We can consider that, as with Enkidu, Huwawa actually existed, per the view of the ancient scribe penning the Epic. Like Enkidu, Huwawa, also called Humbaba, represents a hybrid-hominid creature too. More information on hybrid-hominid evolution and hidden histories are available in the upcoming New Muse Series book, *Ancient Shock ~ Monsters, Philosophers, & Saviors ~ How Neanderthals Became Sapiens.*

Generally speaking, a hybrid-hominid refers to an ancient creature that had a greater Neanderthal-Sapiens DNA admixture, as compared to the 1–5% Neanderthal DNA in modern humans.)

Tablet VII: The Death of Enkidu

nkidu's sickness progresses, and he has a feverish dream where the Gods of the Cedar Forest take counsel, in order to assess the killing of Huwawa, which they see as a senseless murder. Then Enkidu relates his next dark dream to his good friend, the King.

"And me the fever hath laid on my back.

Why, O my friend, do the great gods now take counsel together?

Gilgamesh hear the dream which I saw in the night.

Enkidu shall die but Gilgamesh shall not die.

Friend, O a dream I have seen in my night-time: the firmament roaring,

Echo'd the earth, and I by myself was standing, when perceived I a man

all dark was his face; his nails like claws of a lion. Me did he overcome,

climbing up; press'd me down, upon me, my body. He seized me,

Me did he lead to the Dwelling of Darkness, the home of Irkalla. Unto the

dwelling from which he who entereth cometh forth never!

Aye, by the road on the passage whereof there can be no returning,

Unto the Dwelling whose tenants are ever bereft of the daylight,

Where for their food is the dust, and the mud is their sustenance: bird-

like. Wear they a garment of feathers: and, sitting there in the darkness,

Never the light will they see.

49

~!~

Enkidu, now near feverish death, continues to relate his dream to his friend, the great King:

On the Gate, when I enter'd, on the house, was humbled the crown, for

those who wore crowns, who of old ruled over the country, 'twas they set

the bakemeats, cool was the water they

served from the skins. When I enter'd into this House of the Dust, were

High Priest and acolyte sitting, seer and magician , the priest who the

sea of the great gods anointed. Here sat the Queen of the Underworld;

she lifted her head and beheld me.

Tablet VIII. The King mourns for his great, fallen friend

At some distant point in the past, a human Sumerian King stood by in tearful vigilance, watching his great friend, Enkidu the Wildman, as he lay dying in bed, with a fevered brow. His red, fur-like hair was now soaked and wet with sweat from the fever. And so Enkidu, the true savior of Uruk's anguished people, silently and finally slipped away beyond the mortal confines of the body.

The author of the Epic is sending a not-so-subtle message to those reading of King Gilgamesh, via the vehicle of Enkidu's dream of dying—*those who wore crowns* in life, would be serving tables in the afterlife, and considered much needed to humble their Egos.

King Gilgamesh and his men return to Uruk, bearing both the lifeless body of Enkidu, and a large load of aromatic cedar trees. Gilgamesh stands before the city's council of elders, with Enkidu's body lying before him . . . and spills his guts:

"Unto me hearken, O Elders, to me, aye, me shall ye listen,

'Tis that I weep for my comrade Enkidu, bitterly crying

51

Like to a wailing woman: my grip is slack'd on the curtle axe

Slung at my thigh, and the brand at my belt from my sight is removed.

Aye, and my festal attire lends naught of its aid for my pleasure,

Me, me hath sorrow assailed, and cast me down in affliction.

Enkidu; we who all overcame, ascending the mountains.

Captured the Heavenly Bull, and destroy'd him: we o'erthrew Huwawa,

He who abode in the Forest of Cedars—O, what is this slumber

Now hath o'ercome thee, for now art thou dark, nor art able to hear me?

Natheless he raised not his eyes, and his heart, when Gilgamesh felt it,

made no beat. The King lifted his voice like a lion; Roar'd like a lioness

robb'd of her whelps. In front of his comrade paced he backwards and

forwards, tearing and casting his ringlets; plucking and casting away all

the grace.

Tablet IX: Gilgamesh, in Terror of Death, Seeks Eternal Life

The hideous lament of Gilgamesh for his fallen comrade is so great that he literally pulls his hair out, while screaming and ignoring the great pain.

All throughout the night, the sobbing, growling King paces by the bed of his now-released friend. The next morning, at the break of dawn, Gilgamesh makes bold new plans and addresses the red, dead body of Enkidu.

"O, on a couch of great size will I, thy friend and thy brother,

Gilgamesh, grant thee to lie, on a handsome couch will I grant thee

rest, and to sit on a throne of great size, a throne at my left hand,

so that the princes of Hades may kiss thy feet in their homage;

I, too, will make all the people of Erech lament in thy honour,

Making them mourn thee and damsels and heroes constrain to thy

service, While I myself for thy sake, will cause my body to carry

stains, and will put on the skin of a lion, and range o'er the desert."

The sense of adventure changes dramatically as the King ponders deeply upon both life and death, after Enkidu is killed by the Gods of the Cedar Forest. All this in revenge against Gilgamesh for killing their beloved monster, Huwawa. The Epic poem tells the outer story of a young hero contending with Gods and demons, as well as grappling with key issues that still confound us today: how to deal with the grief of a deceased loved one, the meaning of existence, and the great fear of death.

William Somerset Maugham, the great 19th-century author, referred to this harsh awakening as the shattering of the 'immortality of youth,' where a realization of death suddenly dawns upon the emerging mind entering adulthood. After Enkidu dies of a slow, debilitating illness, Gilgamesh seeks out a man named Utnapishtim, for advice concerning obtaining eternal life, and thus avoiding death. We further discuss new, provocative ideas concerning Utnapishtim in an upcoming segment.

"Gilgamesh bitterly wept for his comrade, for Enkidu, ranging

Over the desert: "I, too—shall I not die like Enkidu also?

Sorrow hath enter'd my heart; I fear death as I range o'er the desert,

I will get hence on the road to the presence of Uta-Napishtim."

Our purpose here is to avoid the outer, academic interpretation of the Epic, and instead, focus on the lesser-known, but even more curious details in the ancient poem—details that have been overlooked for thousands of years. These details, that may reveal a hidden, neuropsychological, even mystical nature to King Gilgamesh, seem poetically and symbolically 'encrypted' in the twelve tablets of the Epic. As in other poetic literature, both old and new, we may fully expect the devious, playful poets to make full use of multiple plots and the play of double entendre as they encrypt their various meanings, which often contain a spiritual underpinning. Joseph Campbell knew this poetical ploy well and spoke of it often. The 'Poetic Edda' literature of the 10th century Norse Vikings is one such encrypted example, where deep Yogic ideas are poetically and symbolically spun into Northern prose and verse. Numerous supporting details are provided in another New Muse Series book, entitled, *The Vikings Secret Yoga ~ The Supreme Adventure.*

Chapter 5 ~ He Who Saw the Deep

Whoever wrote the poetic story of this ancient King used its very title to reveal their deepest metaphysical meaning. The Epic of Gilgamesh is also known as: *Sha naqba īmuru*; *He Who Saw the Deep,* or, in another translation: *He who Sees the Unknown.*

Suddenly, with this alternative translation of the poem's name, we can see the ancient poet's true psychological thrust, of a human King going through the phases of youthful egotism, the death of friendship, and then transcending, in his psychic insight, into 'the deep' or 'the unknown.' Nearly all cultures, both old and new, exhibit languages and literatures where a human, either woman or man, meets mysteriously with their deeper nature. In other words, a human meets their deep primordial God. The Bible's verse, *Be still and know that I am God,* may be considered another poetical vehicle to describe the nature of the relation of the Ego to the much deeper nature of humankind, which, indeed, is God-like, according to Hindu and other Eastern literature. If only the left-brained Ego would shut up, the neural Wisdom Body would respond, in its own cultural way! This seemingly psychological translation of the poem's name causes much consternation for many a scholar, who thus might favor the outer storyline of the King and Enkidu, much of which may have been intended for the masses as folk or children's tales, as in the Norse Bard's Poetic Edda. In all ages, great poets tend to keep their best secrets well hidden from profane eyes. "He Who Saw the Deep" may have been an intended allegory.

The Gilgamesh Epic also has a strange-sounding author—***Sin-Leqi-Unninni***, whose name translates to *Moon God, accept my plea.* Thus, we don't know the anonymous poet's true name, as if he or she were deliberately hiding their identity, while acknowledging a deep, nighttime prayer of remorse. The author's name, given in the form of a prayer, would have been in direct response to the evil youthful days of King Gilgamesh, when he greatly oppressed his people by slavery and rape. ***Sin-Leqi-Unninni*** may have been a woman, anguished for her children, and venting her tears to the Moon Above.

In the Epic of Gilgamesh, there are many sub-plots' stories and elements that remained unexplained; in this small space we seek only to address a few anomalies . . . such as why Gilgamesh is considered one-third human and two-thirds God. The meaning of this personal, kingly division has puzzled scholars for centuries. Normally, they expect a God-and-human sexual mating to produce hybrid children that are considered half-God and half-human, such as the Greek Heracles. Gilgamesh breaks rank and delves into human and divine 'thirds.'

It's easy to get lost in the chase of the many broken Epic of Gilgamesh tablets, however, if we continue to observe the association of ancient literature with neural aspects and traits involved with our representation of the three, distinct brains in the human cranium, we may arrive at a new, symbolic answer to the Epic poet's curious encryption. Throughout the entire New Muse book series, we portray numerous cultures—the Greeks, Hindus, Egyptians, Aztecs, etc.—as all having an innate, intuitive understanding of the integrated neural system, which we may also call the Wisdom Body, since that was a favored phrase of Joseph Campbell, in describing the deepest nature of our body and mind. In earlier pages we revealed that the human body consists of many interacting neural components, and somehow, the anonymous author of the world's oldest poem also knew this, yet described it poetically, not in terms of neuroscience and brain-lateralization. We will attempt to do so now and thus explain the curious and unexplained description of Gilgamesh as one-third Man (Ego) and two-thirds God:

"Who is there can rival his kingly standing, and say like Gilgamesh,

"It is I am the King"? Gilgamesh was his name from the day he was

born, two-thirds of him god and one-third human."

King Gilgamesh was a recurring character in many other Mesopotamian stories and myths, but only in the Epic of *He Who Saw the Deep* is the *one-third to two-third ratio* of Man to God mentioned. Archaeologists and linguistic scholars try to interpret this unfathomable ratio as somehow belonging to a superior demi-God, but there is much more detail to consider. As we know, our Ego is housed mainly in the left hemisphere and is usually extremely dominant, to the detriment of the remaining intelligences of the Wisdom Body, which are considered unconscious. As the evolving, possibly suffering Ego peers across the connecting corpus callosum into the right hemisphere, a type of divinity may be sensed, or, alternatively, nothing at all. A dominant Ego can occlude any spiritual connection, even if they are nearby. It concentrates on itself for its survival. It is an orphan. If a person often feels this way, and is lonely, it is likely because of their falling into a left-brain-dominant mindset, which occludes all realities, save its own. Being spiritually open-minded can restore balance. As stated earlier, it is well known in neuroscience that there are differing traits and dramatic differences between the left and the right brain hemispheres. As was discussed before, one of the most crucial, yet little known traits is the length of the neuron arms. The right hemisphere has far superior neural reach, as contrasted with the left hemi-field, in that the arms of its neurons, (the dendrites and axons) are significantly longer and reach deeply into 'non-contiguous' tissue, meaning the older portions of the brain, the limbic and reptilian locations. The left hemisphere, with its neurons having short axons and dendrites, cannot extend into the deeper tissues of the rear brain as the right brain can. Another important trait of the right hemisphere is that it houses the intelligence that sees 'living sentiency' in other creatures. The world becomes alive if we are whole-brained in our approach.

Can't You See It's All Alive?

Bring It On; Seal

Since we are discussing sentiency in the outside world, it's extremely important to include internal sentience; those other, governing, primordial intelligences living and working in the human skull, heart and body. Without internal sentience, and the greater knowledge of oneself, as Body, Mind & Spirit, spiritual failure is inevitable. Socrates and the Oracle at Delphi advised others to 'Know Thy Self,' but Pythagoras had stated it earlier, more succinctly:

'Know the Empire of Thy Self'

Our ancient Sumerian poet may have somehow obtained intuitive knowledge of the three 'governors' of the human brain, as they are known to modern neuroscience and cleverly portrayed them in the great Epic.

One of these neural governors was referred to as King Gilgamesh the Man by our astute poet; this is Man as the outward-facing Ego. The other two neural governors, namely the right hemisphere and the rear brain cerebellum, were known to 'house' the deity or deities in man; thus, Gilgamesh was two-thirds God.

The ancient poet's secret intention was to portray the King as representing all of humanity, since they too, are mortal and God in one being. This is the true saga; we, as sages, are literally Body, Mind & Spirit. We, as Ego, look outside of ourselves for answers.

Joseph Campbell once commented that, to paraphrase, we ourselves are the answer, yet the Ego doesn't understand, and asks relentless questions as to the nature of reality, which, in the deepest sense, it already is. The Wisdom Body may appear in the beginning as a labyrinth to the Ego, as it awakens. In this author's opinion, there is a fairly well-hidden *neural understanding* that has flowed down through the ages, that has eluded the public and academic eye, but perhaps may have survived in medieval European secret societies such as the Freemasons, Rosicrucians, and others. As a quick example, several neurologists have recently pointed out that clever signs of neural depictions are actually painted into the famous painting of 'The Creation of Adam,' by Michelangelo himself, on the ceiling of the Sistine Chapel. It takes great spiritual knowledge and enormous courage to make such a marvelous and artful statement; thus, Michelangelo must have been a cunning devil, as he successfully fooled the Christian Fathers for centuries. More details concerning Michelangelo, and other artists in this neurals-as-art regard, are found in the upcoming New Muse Series book, *The Color of Minds in the Garden of Knowledge*.

Another example of medieval knowledge of neural processes comes from Emmanuel Swedenborg, the great 18th-century Swedish scientist-philosopher, who wrote the following statement concerning the rear brain:

"...And the influx of celestial angels is into that part of the head which covers the cerebellum, and is called the occiput, extending from the ears in all directions even to the back of the neck; for that region corresponds to **wisdom***"*

(Occiput' is simply an older scientific term, referring to the rear of the brain.)

Even though thousands of years separates the Epic of Gilgamesh from Michelangelo and Swedenborg, the neuro-spiritual message seems the same, or at least very similar. All humans are like Adam and Gilgamesh— we are neurally wired for success if we surrender the dominant attitude (Ego) to the reality of divine neuro-spiritual integration, knowing thyself as the Wisdom Body.

Together, the right brain, with its long reach of its neural arms, is neurally connected to the rear brain. To the ancient mystics, this may have been seen as a continuous, enhanced vast awareness. This 'potentially' vast awareness is connected to our neural, dynamically pulsing heart, which can be referred to as our 'hidden' God consciousness, which is beyond Maya, Man, and the Gods.

Thus, the allegorical Gilgamesh was a Man because of his left-brained Ego, yet a God because of the deep connecting nature of right and rear brains. The legend of one-third Man and two-thirds God, as King Gilgamesh, can be seen as yet another ancient, symbolic reference to man's true human and divine nature, if awakened.

In this case, at over 4,000 years old, it is the oldest poetical reference to our divine nature. Further, the Enuma Elish, the Sumerian creation verses, also clearly state that the body of man is considered God-like:

In the clay, god and man

59

Shall be bound,

To a unity brought together;

So that to the end of days

The Flesh and the Soul

Which in a god have ripened –

That soul in a blood-kinship be bound.

Let us remember that, in the Epic of Gilgamesh, both the King and the Wildman are said to have been formed from clay. This is an ancient description of evolving Body, Mind & Spirit. We also recall the Hindu legend of the great man-God creature; the Nara-Narayana.

We can find more ancient literature that indicates knowledge of Human-and-God relations in their spiritual approach, as being related to the human neural system.

The Neural AUM

Now, *revealed for the first time in history,* we will show that the extremely popular, sacred AUM of the Hindu Upanishads, as seen below in Devanagari script form, has a decidedly neural aspect, since the ancient descriptions of traits, is also matched by identical neuroscience attributes, as shown below. The symbolism is indeed surreal.

The Hindu Devanagari script depicting A U M

The lower three connected curves represent the three neural governors, beyond which, is a bar-curve representing 'Maya,' and behind is the Heart.

"Now this the Self, as to the imperishable Word, is OM; and as to

the letters, His parts are the letters and the letters are his parts,

namely, A U M.

The Waker, *Vishwa, the Universal Male, He is A, the first letter.*

The Dreamer, *Taijasa, the Inhabitant in Luminous Mind, He is U,* *the second letter.*

The Sleeper, *Prajna, the Lord of Wisdom, He is M the third letter."*

The sound of a chanted AUM produces traveling brain waves which resonate with the natural breathing of the heart, lungs and body. The AUM represents audible, primordial letters that provide a vibratory access path to our deepest inner nature. It's important to remember what Shankara, the great yogin of the 8th century AD stated concerning the nature of self as related to the AUM:

> *"The Entity Which Cognizes,*
>
> *Enters into the Three Conditions*
>
> *One after Another and not Simultaneously."*

The Entity, or conscious energy, moving through these conditions may be considered, in neuroscience terms, as a conscious traveling wave moving rapidly throughout the three neural governors. With a new, alternative explanation, we can produce a definite link between the ancient sound and symbol of AUM to our neural depictions, as follows:

Each of the AUM symbol's three lower connected 'curves' have specific meanings. The Ego is represented as the outward-faced Waker; this is the left-brain portrayal, known to neuroscience as the Self-Module.

The Dreamer curve can be associated with our right hemisphere, which is, in modern times, neurologically known to dream, as opposed to the left brain, which does not. The AUM's Sleeper curve is associated with the rear brain, which psychology may refer to as the deep unconscious; yet this Sleeper may be awakened, if a Yogini or Yogin is successful in their efforts. The Sleeper has Divine Potential. Thus, the Waker, Dreamer, and Sleeper represent the three cranial brain-minds. Now, what follows is particularly interesting.

The Devanagari AUM symbol has, at the top, another curve, behind which is a Diamond. This upper curve represents Maya, or the idea of illusion, in the Hindu system. Beyond Maya, the Diamond represents the Heart Center, the hidden, fourth state of sublime consciousness to which all Yogins and Yoginis retreat, having silenced the opposing, chattering Waker—the brain-mind of the Ego. Thus, the Heart Center is considered beyond the illusion of phantasmagoric Maya which the three brains participate in. We call this everyday reality, which is always abuzz and enticing the Ego to embrace its desires, by firing its left-brain neurons, and enjoying its dopamine transmitter, which is associated with the Ego's desires. This is why the Ego's desire can cause a person to become left-brain-dominant, as was King Gilgamesh in his youth.

To the ancient Yogin, the Heart Center was the abode of the Absolute Deity. The brains in the head were considered as a type of observing 'periscope,' forever looking into Maya, for the neural, beating Heart, hidden deep in the body. The Heart represents Turyia, the fourth state of consciousness, or what may be called pure energy-intelligence.

Both the ancient and modern observations of heart-brain relations are remarkably similar, although couched in different phrases.

HeartMath Institute (see www.heartmath.org) is the leading organization in the world today, that studies heart, brain, and electromagnetic interactions, in both a scientific and a highly spiritual way.

With these neuro-spiritual observations of AUM, we should consider that AUM must always be chanted with great awe. Today, many layfolk often trivialize the sound and meaning of AUM as being fairly meaningless and never penetrate into its depths.

It seems at least some of the ancient peoples were 'neural intuitive' and referred to the different neural areas by their dynamic character traits, which worked well as an approach to a Body, Mind & Spirit system. Contrastingly, mainstream neuroscience's modus operandi is to see the entire human body system in terms of its working parts—a reductionist view with severe limitations, which consistently moves away from, and even abhors, the thought of wholeness.

This ancient 3-brain 'psychological scenario' we describe here as AUM, is only slightly akin to, and not to be confused with, the strictly clinical Triune Brain hypothesis put forward by neurologist Paul MacLean in the 1960s. In MacLean's theory, the Triune Brain's three components are considered the frontal lobes (both hemispheres) and the rear limbic, and reptilian areas. The Triune brain hypothesis, while having an important clinical value as to brain function, is slightly different in its focus. Our neural approach here is to appreciate the long-armed connections between the right hemisphere and the rear brain area, which can be seen, or seem as also being closely associated, in a mysterious way, to the Heart Center and the Wisdom Body itself. These can appear as one entity, or several, to the orphaned Ego.

We can look more deeply into the nature of our being, as did Gilgamesh, and even become one who 'Knows the Deep.'

~!~

Before we dismiss the Epic of Gilgamesh's outer storyline as a simple, primitive ancient myth, we must listen very closely to the ancient poet-scribes who were subtly leaving traces of their own beliefs, and that of ancient Sumerian Culture. Although historical information is sparse, King Gilgamesh is often considered as one of the Ten Kings in the Sumerian King List. This list, comprised of cuneiform writing upon a single large stone tablet, outlines a curious, semi-mythical history of their long-lived Kings, many of which lived for thousands of years, similar to those extremely aged patriarchs of the Bible. Once again, religious (Christian) plagiarism is suspected and is highly likely.

Gilgamesh may be allegorical, or he may yet be historical. Regardless, in the Epic, we are really dealing with the ancient author; we follow the poet's view and stanzas, not that of the King, who is simply the voice of the poet-scribe. In many Sumerian stories, Gilgamesh is said to be the son of the Sumerian goddess Ninsun and King Lugalbanda, which seems simple enough as creation myths generally go, but in the tablets of the Sumerian King list, we find Gilgamesh is mysteriously listed as the son of 'the Phantom Lord of Uruk.' This leaves yet another path to consider as most Mesopotamian cities and countries, such as Uruk, had their own invisible, sovereign Lord or God.

Another potential encryption, as an allegorical reference to the Wisdom Body, may be seen in the Epic's original title, which translates as *Surpassing All Other Kings* (Shutur eli sharri). This title shifted to *He Who Saw the Deep* (Sha naqba imuru) in later Sumerian versions. Most scholars take the phrase of *Surpassing All Other Kings* as an egotistical reference that simply compares Gilgamesh to the other Kings on the Sumerian Kings list, but there may be a deeper explanation, if we recall that Gilgamesh is one-third Man and two-thirds God. Could it be that Gilgamesh, as one-third Man, or left-brained Ego, looked into his deeper nature, which is seen as divinely alive? This is his Wisdom Body that he looked into, which is the two-thirds God; the neural concert of right hemisphere, rear brain, and the heart center. Anyone who does this with great persistence and sincerity will 'see the deep,' even today, but there are few, since humanity is over ninety percent left-brain-dominant, or Ego-driven, and religion today is nearly dead, as compared to the ancients.

The sacred message of the Epic of Gilgamesh remains quite true today as a revelation of Body, Mind & Spirit, however, our society is entering a new phase of turmoil. Spirituality is a minor current today, as the world burns and spins into a raucous, mentally degraded environment, ruled by the King of Pain, the runaway Ego. Thus, we are on the path that Iain McGilChrist noted; the idea of a powerful 'Emissary-Ego,' like King Gilgamesh, is portrayed as a runaway psychological force that ultimately degrades or destroys the entire known world.

As is seen in numerous esoteric literature in many cultures, if the Ego (one-third) will sincerely submit (Islam) or surrender itself, then the separation of existence disappears as the Wisdom Body becomes complete, while the Ego peers into the amazing, deep Gateway that is only seen by the spiritually awakened who are gathering divine experience. Perhaps the author of the Epic is suggesting that, because of his man-God nature, Gilgamesh could be seen as an ancient sage-King, or philosopher-King, where great wisdom, especially that concerning life and death, is seen embodied in the ruler.

Thus, after his trials, and having gained spiritual wisdom, Gilgamesh could be seen as *Surpassing All Other Kings* . . . but this was after the evil excesses of his youth.

Perhaps one could say, after you see 'The Deep,' you surpass any earth-bound Kings. To use Christian jargon, a person could inwardly experience 'The King of Kings,' where the inner Holiness is referred to as Christ. In a Hindu view, the 'one-third Man' can be seen as the 'little self' or Ego of the left brain, while the Great Self (the Deep or Unknown) enters the human sphere by the combined efforts of the right and rear brains working in combination to influence and assist the separated 'little self' of the great, yet humble God-King. Once Gilgamesh matured beyond his hellish youth, he became a wise teacher.

Below, a great 'secret' is mentioned: this is how important the ancient poet considers the Man-and-God concept of a true King, who conquers himself:

"He who, the heart of all matters hath proven, let him teach the nation,

He who all knowledge possesseth, therein shall he school all the people,

He shall his wisdom impart, and so shall they share it together.

Gilgamesh, he was the Master of wisdom, with knowledge of all things.

He 'twas discovered the secret concealed.

Two-thirds of him are divine, and one-third of him human."

Tablet I, the Epic of Gilgamesh

In another jargon, after the trying times of youth and the realization of unavoidable death, the adult King Gilgamesh can be seen as a deeply 'self-realized' person, a ruler who surrenders his Ego to the Greater Ruler inside and by doing so, 'sees the Deep.' Taking this inside alternative approach can provide important psychological and spiritual answers to the mysterious writings of the ancient author-poet. Taking the outer view of Gilgamesh as a mythical King, without consideration of the subtle touch of the poet, renders and degenerates the Epic into a fairy tale for the children and the masses. All subtle meanings are lost. This notion of finding secondary, moralistic plots in the Epic is not new, however, much of the information presented in this book is unique and original—previously unseen.

Chapter 6 ~ Terror, Death, and the Quest for Eternal Life

Before he died, Enkidu had an immensely powerful dream which he related to his friend Gilgamesh. In the dream, Enkidu witnesses the details of his own death, complete with an Underworld journey, where he encountered the Queen of Hades, a character the Greeks later employed in their own myth. In 'The House of Dust,' the realm of the dead, a terrifying creature, part man, lion, and bird, approaches him and sinks his talons into Enkidu and begins to drag him below:

"Me did he lead to the Dwelling of Darkness, the home of Irkalla,

Unto the Dwelling from which he who entereth cometh forth never!

Aye, by the road on the passage . . . whereof there can be no returning."

The outer storyline of the Great Epic reveals that after the sudden, painful death of Enkidu, Gilgamesh's great true friend and companion, the King goes through several psychological changes. If we begin to look into the Sumerian poet's secret, inner initiative of story development, this may be seen as representative of all mankind. Firstly, the King grieves with great intensity, roaring like a lion at the world as he laments over Enkidu's dead body. Then, as Gilgamesh realizes that Death will also come for him and he becomes overwhelmed with the terrorizing prospect of his own demise, he starts to live in continuous fear of death. Thirdly, Gilgamesh begins a marvelous journey to determine if Eternal Life can be obtained, and thus avoiding Death. He seeks out Utnapishtim—an Immortal Human.

"And Gilgamesh bitterly wept for his comrade, Enkidu, ranging over the

desert: "I, too—shall I not die like Enkidu also? Sorrow hath enter'd my

heart; I fear death as I range o'er the desert, I will get hence on the road to the presence of Utnapishtim...with speed will I travel... 'tis in darkness

that I shall arrive at the Gates of the Mountains."

Tablet IX, The Epic of Gilgamesh

As we read about Gilgamesh weeping inconsolably at the death of his hybrid wild friend 4,000 years ago, I am strangely reminded of a modern epic—that of Star Trek, where in one scene, Captain James T. Kirk weeps at the death of his hybrid Vulcan friend; an honest man called Spock. The eulogy he delivers might well have been the words of our sobbing Sumerian King:

> *"Of all the Souls I have encountered in my Travels,*
>
> *his was the most human"*

~!~

Let's consider the poetic meaning of the name-translations once more:

Gilgamesh: Surpassing all other Kings, He Who Saw the Deep.

Utnapishtim: The Faraway, The Distant, considered the Immortal One.

At this middle stage, Gilgamesh is unaccomplished and has not risen to the spiritual heights as his name implies, yet he is terrified of death.

> *He doesn't care to wake up to the nightmare that's become real life*

You Haven't Done Nothin'; Stevie Wonder

The story of the Kings quest to meet 'he who is far away, or distant' reveals much of the richer, inner storyline desired to be revealed by the ancient poet, but first we must detail the given, outer storyline.

Casting away all of his old vanity and pride, Gilgamesh sets out on a quest to find the meaning of life and, finally, some way of defeating death. In doing so, he becomes the first epic hero in world literature. The remorse of Gilgamesh, and the questions his friend's death evoke, resonate with every human being who has struggled with the meaning of life in the face of death. After traveling a long distance, Gilgamesh arrives at the guarded, spiritual gates of the mountains where the immortal Utnapishtim, along with his wife, is said to dwell.

"Mashu the name of the hills; as he reached the Mountains of Mashu,

Where every day they keep watch o'er the Sun-god's rising and setting.

Unto the Zenith of Heaven uprear'd are their summits, and downwards

deep unto Hell."

In the Epic, Utnapishtim (The Faraway-Distant) and his wife are the sole immortals amongst the humans. Their immortality was bestowed as a gift of thanks from the Gods during the Great Flood, where Utnapishtim, like Noah, preserves humanity and many animals in his boat, aptly named, *The Preserver of Life*. Gilgamesh is desperate to learn of a method by which he too may escape death; thus, the King wants to live forever.

However, at the portal of the Gateway Mountains stand sentries; Scorpion-men, awful in terror, whose very glance is Death. There is a brief, spoken exchange between the traveling King and the Scorpion-men in which the following words are traded:

"Lo, he that cometh to us—'tis the flesh of the gods is his body.

Two parts of him god-like, only a third of him human"

In the prose of the ninth tablet of the Epic, a Scorpion-man addresses Gilgamesh, asking him why he has traveled on such a tedious journey. Gilgamesh informs the Scorpion-men that his purpose is to ask Utnapishtim how to become, like he and his wife, immortal in the flesh. But another Scorpion-man speaks up and responds by informing him that such a thing is impossible, and that a journey like that has never been made across the Gateway mountains. Nevertheless, perhaps taken on as a hero's trial, Gilgamesh is also briefed by the Scorpion-men, that there is a perilous, 24-hour journey which is referred to as 'The Road to the Sun.' This begins in total darkness and ends with seeing the full blaze of the Sun, where one may behold the Tree of the Gods, which is considered the Vine of Life, thus springing from the Sun. The King listens carefully but decides to embark on the quest, and the Scorpion-men wish him well on his difficult task. As the King starts out upon his questionable journey, and perhaps gazes into the morning sunrise, Shamash, the Sun-God, suddenly appears to Gilgamesh and speaks:

"Gilgamesh, never a crossing shall be where none hath been ever,

No, so long as the gale driveth water.

Gilgamesh, why dost thou run, for the Life

which Thou seekest, Thou shalt not find."

Shamash is informing Gilgamesh that eternal life in the physical body will not be possible for him. Undaunted, the King speaks his own mind to Shamash concerning his quest for eternal life:

"Shall I, after I roam up and down o'er the waste as a wand'rer,

Lay my head in the bowels of earth, and throughout the years slumber

Ever and aye? Let mine eyes see the Sun and be sated with brightness,

Yea, for the darkness is banish'd afar, if wide be the brightness.

When will the man who is dead ever look on the light of the Sunshine?"

At this critical juncture, let us pause in the telling of the outer storyline to reflect upon an important psychological distinction of which the ancient poet will soon be unveiling.

71

As we have seen, the Ego portion of humankind's brain, the left hemisphere, is heavily involved in the desire for eternal life. Hope and optimism are heavily favored by the left-brain, and it's easy to see that our purely Ego-centered self, like the young, immature Gilgamesh, would love to pursue a life of physical immortality. This was also the quest of the 15th-century Spanish Conquistadors led by Juan Ponce De Leon, where they foolishly sought a Fountain of Youth in the newly founded Americas. This endless quest for eternal life in the physical world is something which many scientists in the modern world aspire to, and they continuously attempt to develop the technological capability to do so. This is one of the strongest desires in the history of humankind, yet it is the incorrect method or path . . . and doomed to fail.

Let us be clear: Gilgamesh is usually seen by scholars as actually failing in his quest for eternal life, but this is only the outer storyline and much has been overlooked. Because Gilgamesh, like ourselves, is one-third human and two-thirds God, he will actually succeed . . . just not in the desired Egotistical sense. It is imperative to relax and disengage our Ego, and reach into our deeper nature, which, according to the deepest of Yogic traditions, truly is God-like.

I feel that the ancient Sumerian poet, is subtly informing us using his inner, symbolic, and secretive storyline, which most analytic scholars and the lay public do not detect. The inner Gilgamesh saga is truly one for the ages; one learns how to drop the Ego, connect with the Deep, and thus overcome Death. This beautiful, rare and marvelous process has been reflected countless times in the known history of the world and its religions—the Song remains the Same. It is Yoga. It is basic Jungian psychology. It is the endless story of the little (s) and large (S) selves, which Ralph Waldo Emerson described as Soul and Over-Soul.

As Gilgamesh continues his querulous journey into the mountains to find eternal life, he next encounters the veiled Siduri, the goddess of enchantment, ale, and wine, and perhaps the elixir of Soma. Here we extract from the Tenth Epic tablet;

"There dwelt Siduri, the maker of wine, Cover'd she was with a veil.

Gilgamesh wander'd towards her; Pelts was he wearing

Flesh of the gods in his body possessing, *but woe in his belly,*

Aye, and his countenance like to a man who hath gone a far journey."

Gilgamesh is looking extremely forlorn, depressed, and dangerous. Having lost his best friend, he has nothing in the world to live for and is terrified of his own death. Spying his approach, Siduri quickly bars her house door but it's too late—the weary King has noticed her and bangs upon her door, and threatens to break it down. The goddess-witch relents, and a dialog ensues where Gilgamesh vigorously denies his forlorn condition and vents his troubles of woe to Siduri and recaps his tales of adventure with Enkidu. Siduri, like Shamash earlier, also attempts to dissuade the depressed King from pursuing his quest for eternal life:

"Gilgamesh, why runnest thou, in as much as the life which thou seekest,

Thou canst not find? For the gods, in their first creation of mortals,

Death allotted to man, but life they retain'd in their keeping.

Gilgamesh, full be thy belly, each day and night be thou merry, and daily

keep holiday revel, each day and night do thou dance and rejoice; and

fresh be thy raiment. Aye, let thy head be clean washen, and bathe thyself

in the water, Cherish the little one holding thy hand; thy spouse in thy

bosom, Be Happy, for this is the dower of man."

Gilgamesh, however, is undeterred by Siduri's words of living a simple, pleasurable, ordinary life and presses on. He inquired of the Goddess:

"Pr'ythee, then, Wine-maker, which is the way unto Utnapishtim?

What is its token? I pr'ythee, vouchsafe me, vouchsafe me its token.

If it be possible even the Ocean itself will I traverse,

But if it should be impossible, then will I range o'er the desert."

~!~

Per our poet's inner intent, Gilgamesh is told once more that there is no such path to 'the faraway' eternal life for humankind:

"Thus, did the Wine-maker answer to him, unto Gilgamesh saying,

"There hath been never a crossing, O Gilgamesh: never aforetime

Anyone, coming thus far, hath been able to traverse the Ocean:

Warrior Shamash doth cross it, 'tis true, but who besides Shamash

Maketh the traverse? Yea, rough is the ferry, and rougher its passage,

Aye, too, 'tis deep are the Waters of Death, which bar its approaches.

Ur-Shanabi; Boatman of the Immortal One, the Waters of Death

At this point, after hearing that it is only the Sun-Warrior in the sky above that can successfully traverse the vast Ocean, the Sumerian poet begins to move further into the inner storyline, which is rich with intended, encrypted symbolism. The Ocean and all Epic characters become symbolic. Therefore, after being repeatedly told by the Scorpion-men, the Goddess of Wine, and then the Sun-God, that there is no path to his desired immortality, suddenly, in a great reversal, Gilgamesh is subsequently informed that *there is indeed a path . . .* and it starts with a special boatman who can traverse the 'Waters of Death' and finally take the King to 'The Faraway' (Utnapishtim). The goddess Siduri continues:

"Gilgamesh, if perchance thou succeed in traversing the Ocean,

What wilt thou do, when unto the Waters of Death thou arrivest?

75

Gilgamesh, there is Ur-Shanabi, boatman to Uta-Napishtim,

He with whom sails are, the **urnu** *of which in the forest he plucketh,*

Now let him look on thy presence, and if it be possible with him

Cross...but if it be not, then do thou retrace thy steps homewards."

Generally, scholars are unsure of the meaning of 'urnu,' but we will provide an explanation shortly. The reader may notice that Ur-Shanabi, the Epic's boatman on the untouchable River of Death, will later be absorbed into the Greek notions of Hades and Charon, the boatman who can cross the river Styx. Sizable portions of Tablet 10 are unreadable, and we next find Gilgamesh meeting the boatman, Ur-Shanabi, in quest of the Distant One:

"Then did Ur-Shanabi speak to him yea, unto Gilgamesh, saying:

"Tell to me what is thy name, for I am Ur-Shanabi, henchman,

Aye, of far Uta-Napishtim." To him did Gilgamesh answer:

"Gilgamesh, that is my name, come hither from Erech.

One who hath traversed the Mountains, a wearisome journey of Sunrise,

Now that I look on thy face, Ur-Shanabi—Uta-Napishtim

Let me see also—the Distant one!" Him did Ur-Shanabi answer.

Gilgamesh, thus did Ur-Shanabi speak to him, yea, unto Gilgamesh,

saying "Why is thy vigour all wasted?"

Let's remember that, in addressing the boatman, the King's name should be translated as either 'Surpassing all Kings' or 'He Who Saw the Deep.'

Gilgamesh ignores the boatman's question and repeats his statement that he will traverse the Ocean or the Desert to find the immortal Utnapishtim. It's important to note that the usual interpretation of Gilgamesh's condition, or wasted vigor, is due to his being completely haggard and in worn-out physical condition—but this is only the outer storyline. In our interpretation, the emphasis of wasted vigor shifts into the state of Gilgamesh's mental and psychological condition. With Enkidu dead and the King in forlorn misery and terrified of death, we can expect to equate the loss of vigor with an extremely depressed mental state.

In this light, vigor can mean 'the spirit of life.' Besides, anyone who can traverse mountains, while fighting animals along the way—as he has done all of his life—must be in pretty good physical shape! The loss of vigor is deeply emotional, not physical, although the King might look like hell. Now, as the saga continues into another broken piece of the tablet, the boatman admonishes Gilgamesh:

"Thus, did Ur-Shanabi speak to him, yea, unto Gilgamesh, saying:

"Gilgamesh, 'tis thine own hand hath hinder'd thy crossing the Ocean.

Thou hast destroyéd the sails(?), (and) hast piercéd (?) the . . .

(Now) destroy'd are the sails(?), and the urnu not .

Although the tablet is fractured, and sentences left incomplete, we can still deduce that the boatman is declaring Gilgamesh to be his own worst enemy. The notion of 'sails and urnu' are seen again in this stanza. We can consider that Ur-Shanabi, as 'the henchmen' of 'The Distant One' has his own sails and urnu intact. It is extremely noteworthy, that this special boatman visits the forest for plant wisdom:

*"He with whom sails are, the **urnu** of which in the forest he plucketh."*

Because the King has no 'Sails or Urnu,' the poet's storyline seemingly shifts again to the outer view, where the boatman simply advises Gilgamesh to go to the forest and build a rude boat of logs which they can use to make the long trip to Utnapishtim's dwelling.

The uneventful trip takes six weeks or more before the pole-boat finally arrives at the symbolic Waters of Death, which the boatman advises Gilgamesh not to touch. Metaphorically, by having no sails of his own, the King is reduced to using multiple poles to slowly and tediously thrust the boat forward.

The Immortal One, Utnapishtim, spies their approach and once more sees that Gilgamesh's psychological state is unhealthy. He has no 'internal' sails, and therefore, cannot soar into the Deep.

"Uta-Napishtim look'd into the distance and, inwardly musing,

Said to himself: "Now, why are the sails of the vessel destroyed?

Aye, and one who is not of my . . . (?) doth ride on the vessel?

This is no mortal who cometh: nor . . . .

I look, but this is no mortal. . . . . . "

Although the tablet is broken and only partially decipherable, we can consider that 'The Distant One,' Utnapishtim, sees that 'the sails of the vessel' are destroyed or non-existent, in reference to Gilgamesh's psychological state. Furthermore, he seems to recognize that the King is no mere mortal, perhaps this a further reference to Gilgamesh's Wisdom Body, which renders him one-third Man and two-thirds God. The King himself doesn't seem to understand his own divine nature, nor the notion that his 'sails' are damaged; the poet may be trying to indicate that Gilgamesh is in an unconscious state and not aware of his own divine potential. He cannot say, "soar with the eagles"—not yet. Upon their first meeting, the King regales Utnapishtim with the long stories of his wearisome and difficult travels, all made in order to find immortal life.

Another Tale of Two Birds

Epic Tablet 10, with its broken status, concludes with a few mysterious lines, but we are not sure if it is Utnapishtim or Gilgamesh who, in a deep philosophical sense, speaks:

"Shall we forever build houses, forever set signet to contract,

Brothers continue to share, or among foes always be hatred?

Or will forever the stream that hath risen in spate bring a torrent,

Kulilu bird to Kirippu bird?"

The Sumerian poet seems to be asking if we should be building 'castles in the sand,' which are shared alike by either comrades or by foes-in-hatred. This suggests a dim, illusory outlook on life. Conversely, will the Stream that rises in waves, bring a tsunami? Let's consider the marvelous, lost symbolisms, especially concerning the so-called birds.

Astonishingly, the Kulilu and Kirippu birds may not be birds at all . . . but rather, another poetic encryption by our shrewd, invisible poet.

In reviewing a tome entitled, *A Concise Dictionary of Akkadian*, by Black, George and Postgate, we find that 'Kulilu' actually translates as 'dragonfly' . . . and that ancient definition dramatically reveals our poet's intent.

We go from observing a perceived nonsense, since there is no scholarly understanding as to the Epic's purpose of these two 'birds,' to a great spiritual opportunity, poetically expressed. A dragonfly's transformation process is a bit different from that of the butterfly, which emerges from the chrysalis. The dragonfly nymph-larva molt their skin a dozen times before emerging as an adult. It appears the spiritual molting that modern folks refer to as 'emerging from their chrysalis,' is identical to the misnamed Sumerian Kulilu 'bird,' which is actually a molting dragonfly. The spiritual implication is the same as that of the butterfly. The ancient message is that, while change is endless . . . No One Ever Dies.

And . . . The Endless Song Remains the Same.

Dragonfly on Spiritual Mandala

Nearly all scholars are notoriously silent on the mysterious phrasings concerning these birds, yet, with our alternative explanations, we can continue. The Kirippu 'bird' is also not a bird, but rather a psychological, transcendent state of awareness. In the tome, *The Primeval Flood Catastrophe: Origins and Early Development in Mesopotamian Traditions (Oxford Oriental Monographs)* by Y. S. Chen, published in 2013, we find another potential answer. Y.S. Chen reports that the word 'kirippu' has an ancient meaning of 'the blessed'—a remarkable phrase, which again, turns

80

the Epic of Gilgamesh's symbolism on its hoary head. If we consider the 'Stream' that is mentioned to be the rising stream of unfolding consciousness, then the puzzling, elusive stanzas suddenly click into place. A rising stream of consciousness can launch oneself from the cocoon-like state of the Kulilu 'bird' to marvelously transcend into the Kirippu 'blessed' state. Thus, the cocooned Ego can transform itself as it joins with the transcendent qualities of timelessness known to reside in the right hemisphere.

In ancient cultures, water often symbolically represented mystical birth and renewal. The ancient poet may be subtly informing us that we too can be the molting Kulilu bird—which is then, blessedly, transformed into the transcendent Kirippu bird. Thus, our own human metamorphosis can be completed . . . but we must repeatedly shed the skin of Ego until we rise again, in greater awareness—the blessed form. If we live in the shallows of human awareness, with its focus on materialism and foolish adventures, we destroy our psychological 'sails' which could take us to 'The Deep.'

So, we must be aspirants of our own development, we must know ourselves, and be consciously integrated, to achieve the Blessed State.

Let us recall Dr. Roger Sperry's words here, as being neurally related.

> *"When the brain is whole, the **unified** consciousness of the left*
> *and right hemispheres add up to more than the individual*
> *properties of the separate hemispheres."*

The lack of spiritual awakening due to our misguided thoughts and actions, as in those of the youthful King, could be telling . . . he may plod along with the rest of humanity, until Death is reached.

Tablet 10 concludes with its final stanzas on sunlight, sleep, and death, but once again, we don't know if it's Utnapishtim or the King who is speaking:

"The face which doth look on the sunlight . . . presently shall not be.

Sleeping and dead are alike, from Death they mark no distinction

Servant and master, when once thy have reach'd their full span allotted,

then does the Maker of Destiny with them, doth destiny settle, Death, aye,

and Life they determine; of Death is the day not realéd. "

~!~

So, Sleep has often been called 'the little death' even unto our own times . .
. and the Day of Death continues to be unknown to all.

Chapter 7 ~ The Cosmic Flood of Maya

"After the flood had swept over,
and the kingship had descended
from heaven, the kingship was in Eridu."
The Sumerian King List

~!~

T ablet 11, the so-called 'Flood' tablet of the Epic of Gilgamesh, is one of the most famous pieces, as the scene shifts from focusing on a woeful Gilgamesh, who observes the story of Utnapishtim and how he became immortal. This tablet contains the detailed description of a Great Flood, complete with a Noah's-Ark setting where a huge boat is built, per God's warning of an impending watery deluge, and many animals are saved, etc. As we shall see, there are numerous encrypted meanings in this tablet.

Most western 'religious' scholars purposely ignore the Epic of Gilgamesh, for the sole purpose of protecting their own popular religion. However, nearly all non-Christian experts agree that the great Epic of Sumer's Age was the true forerunner of the Bible's own depiction of the same flood scenario. Cultural diffusion is not rare; there are many flood myths in various religions and teachings. Curiously, in ancient China, we also have a Noah who saves the world after a flood, yet Noah was a female in that legend, apparently created via cultural diffusion, where many things, including sex, often change in the retelling of the original myth.

Earlier, in Tablet 10 of the Epic, a man (Utnapishtim) is seemingly warned by EA, the Sumerian chief deity, to prepare a large vessel for a flood, aka Noah:

"O thou Mortal, Thou of Shurippak, a dwelling pull down,

and fashion a vessel therewith; abandon possessions,

Life do thou seek, and thy hoard disregard, and save life; every creature

make to embark in the vessel. The vessel, which thou art to fashion,

apt be its measure; its beam and its length be in due correspondence,

Then on the deep do thou launch it."

Utnapishtim does as he is told and tears down his house, and uses the materials to fashion a large boat. Later, as the Tempest and Flood abate, Utnapishtim, like Noah, tests for nearby, dry land, using birds:

I open'd a hatchway, and down on my cheek stream'd the sunlight,

Bowing myself, I sat weeping, my tears o'er my cheek(s) overflowing,

Into the distance I gazed, to the furthest bounds of the ocean,

I put forth a dove, and released her, but to and fro went the dove, and

return'd, for a resting-place was not. Then, I a swallow put forth and

released; to and fro went the swallow, She too return'd, for a resting-

place was not; I put forth a raven, her, too, releasing; the raven went,

too, and th' abating of waters saw; and she ate as she waded and

splash'd, unto me not returning. Unto the four winds of heaven I freed all

the beasts, and an off'ring sacrificed, and a libation I pour'd on the peak

84

of the mountain.

The story of the Great Flood, written upon the Eleventh Tablet of the Epic of Gilgamesh, is actually the final tablet in the twelve-tablet series, as generally accepted by modern scholars. The Twelfth tablet was added hundreds of years after the initial imprinting of the Epic, and is incongruous with the preceding tablets, thus it is generally ignored as a late-arriving appendage. For those reasons, we will not be covering Tablet 12, in staying with the original poetic expression over 4,000 years ago. The Eleventh tablet, however, is truly a glorious poetical expression of how Gilgamesh and Utnapishtim can mystically transcend death.

Gilgamesh is Tremendous!

Rainer Maria Rilke

The Eleventh Tablet of the Epic of Gilgamesh is commonly referred to as 'The Flood' and many comparisons are commonly noted between the Akkadian-Sumerian Gilgamesh flood account and the story of the deluge found in the Bible.

The Flood is threat'ning my very life today; Gimme, gimme shelter!

The Rolling Stones

However, the same storyline, that of a great flood, is also continued in other Mesopotamian texts. The Enuma Elish, a Babylonian creation story first written in 1500–1700 BCE, contains numerous flood references similar to Gilgamesh and Genesis of the Bible. The Babylonian Atrahasis Epic, written around the same time, repeatedly mimics the other flood myths. The Chaldean-Babylonian story of 'Ishtar and Izdubar,' written 1200 BCE, 2,500 years after Gilgamesh, contains literally dozens of identical or similar flood references to the earlier poem.

While the continuing saga of a mythical great flood might eventually get boring, especially to scholars, we should note that the inner storylines of these poems seem to largely agree, in many ways, which, if so, is a marvelous continuation. Perhaps each author-poet was initiated into ancient psychological, spiritual tenets, over the many centuries and thus the great beauty of the internal storyline was perpetuated over thousands of years.

In this author's view, the ancient Mesopotamian poet again fancifully weaves several themes into the Epic of Gilgamesh as he crafts his creative, spiritual art piece. The outer storyline is the traditionally accepted ancient story of great deluges. The inner storyline is a spiritual allegory, consisting of hidden metaphors which we will slowly unfold here, and depicts the scene entirely differently—if we can conceptualize the hidden meaning of the 'Flood of Maya.'

Joseph Campbell once coyly commented that Noah himself was a "moon man who had sailed his moon boat on the cosmic sea."

It's certainly true that archaeologists have determined that there was severe river flooding in Mesopotamia in 3000 BCE, around the time of Gilgamesh's kingship; of this we can be sure. The sea-level of the Persian Gulf was 1–2 meters higher than it is today, and its shoreline would have extended 250 miles to the northwest. In ancient times, the ancient city of Ur, just south of Uruk, Gilgamesh's home, was actually listed as a seaport in the various Sumerian tablets. Some scholars have used the word 'tsunami,' indicating that a truly devastating river flooding did occur. Quite truly, many of the Sumerian river folks, and their boats, could have been swept well out to sea. Perhaps some survived, and lived to tell their part, to contribute to the tale of the Great Flood of Sumer.

However, the mythical, massive extrapolation of a biblical flood so huge it would literally wipe out all humankind remains preposterous, even if we go back to the melting of the last Ice Age eleven thousand years ago, which caused massive ocean rises, impacting those on the lower coastlines.

Those who look will never find an old wooden boat on the top of an Akkadian mountaintop, nor will the biblical researchers achieve success in locating Noah's fantastic ship; they are pursuing the delusional myth of a biblical scribe's outer storyline.

On a far lesser scale, let us consider a simpler premise. In the hoary days of old Mesopotamia, one can easily imagine a 'sensitive' man, or his wife, having an intense, precognitive dream where they are warned by a spirit or God, to pack their family and animals into a boat before a local deluge, so violent that river boats were swept out to the nearby large lakes or seas, occurred. The boats being lost at sea for several days, possibly landing near a small rise or hilltop near Mount Nisir, the fabled mountain which supposedly housed the legendary Ark. Mount Nisir can be translated as 'Mount of Salvation,' so a poet's use of double entendre may be present as a poetical distraction, to fool the careless reader in the masses who will only understand the myth of the outer storyline, no matter how meaningless it becomes. Thus, a small dosage of historical deluge in ancient Sumer may serve the poet well, as he surfs into facilitating the underlying, eternally important concept of the cosmic 'Flood of Maya.'

We should recognize that considerable cultural diffusion occurred in 2500 BCE, or before, between two early juggernauts of civilization—namely the Mesopotamian Akkadian-Sumerian cultures, and the nearby Indus Valley people, including the 'Harrapan' folk.

As the Indus Valley developed its spiritual methods, which later developed into Yoga and the Vedas, the important concept of the illusion of earthly life developed into a strong spiritual principle. Calling the oceanic illusion 'Maya,' it also became associated with the idea of sleep, as in an unconscious person moving aimlessly through life, dimly thinking the Earth life is actually real. This ancient psychological notion, which is central to Raja Yoga and Vedanta, could be considered proto-Indo-European, and these mystical ideas may have been exchanged with those in Mesopotamia, via the hoary Steppe Road, the ancient precursor to the Silk Road of later centuries. After deeply understanding the surreal illusion of Maya, then the experience of the deathless, immortal Self may be at the surface upon the mind of the individual. We can still view this rare experience objectively, in consideration of the relations between the Ego in the left hemisphere and the immortality offered through the Wisdom Body of our right and rear cranial brains, in association with the neural wisdom of the Heart and Body. This is also Gilgamesh's human and spiritual situation, with his being one-third Man and two-thirds God.

In this excerpt below from the Mundaka Upanishad, we see a Yogic Experience which is beyond concept, meaning the left-brain Ego cannot 'grasp' the infinity of the Deathless Self.

> *The eye cannot see it; mind cannot grasp it.*
>
> *The Deathless Self has neither caste nor race.*
>
> *Neither eyes nor ears nor hands nor feet.*
>
> *Sages say this Self is infinite in the great*
>
> *and small, everlasting and changeless,*
>
> *The Source of Life.*

Young King Gilgamesh, by his lustful rape of women and love of fighting and killing, has automatically excluded himself, egotistically occluded himself, from his own vast deeper nature. Poetically speaking, he has no 'sails' or wings with which to transcend. It is only due to the impact of meeting and then grieving the death of his good friend Enkidu, that the King begins on his path to awakening and foregoes his former evil habits. As we draw again upon the Indus Valley lore, it's important to note the symbolic use of water-related term in the Epics, such as stream, sea, and ocean, because the Sumerian poet may use them as spiritual metaphors, similar to the Upanishads, as revealed below:

> *"Action prompted by pleasure or profit*
>
> *Cannot help anyone to cross this Sea.*
>
> *Seek a teacher who has realized the Self.*

To a student, whose heart is full of love,

who has conquered his senses and passions,

The Teacher will reveal the Lord of Love."

~!~

With Tablet 11, we note that it is even richer in symbolism, innuendo, and double entendre, than all of the others that precede it. The scene begins with Gilgamesh meeting Utnapishtim and finding him to be physically similar to himself, puzzles the King as to how the 'Faraway-Distant' man obtained his immortality. It is obvious the young King doesn't understand the Deathless Self, which Utnapishtim represents:

"Gilgamesh unto him spake, to Utnapishtim the Distant:

"Utnapishtim, upon thee I gaze, yet in no wise thy presence

Strange is, for thou art like me, and in no wise different art thou;

Thou art like me; O tell me, how couldst thou Stand in the Assemblage

of Gods to petition for life everlasting?"

Utnapishtim, addressing him thus unto Gilgamesh answer'd:

"Gilgamesh, I unto thee will discover the whole hidden story . . .

At this juncture, most of Tablet 11 does indeed go into the great embellishment of the outer flood storyline, complete with boorish details of how to build a large wooden boat and put animals into it, etc. And so, in the Epic, Utnapishtim does indeed spew forth a long, mechanical, detailed saga of how he built his boat, which we review later. He also reveals how the Gods of the city Shurippak, located on the Euphrates river, compelled him to save himself and those around him, from the devastating 'flood.' In the outer myth, and according to scholarly interpretation, Utnapishtim is then considered the sole favorite of the Gods; it was he who listened to them and so survived the great flood. Afterwards, Utnapishtim was rewarded by the Sumer Gods with divinity; he and his wife became immortal.

Fortunately, we can greatly reduce the mystery, and expand the value and meaning of the Epic if we include esoteric and other spiritual analogies here, as shown below. Dr. Muata Ashby, in writing of an ancient Egyptian view, uses words that are similar to those of the ancient scribe of the Epic of Gilgamesh:

The world of unenlightened human existence is likened to being out in the

middle of the ocean when there is a raging storm. The desires are the

waves thrashing the mind about. Spiritual practice is the boat, which

allows a person to weather the storm of the world with its ever-changing

situations. It gives the power to move forward in life and not be disturbed

by the choices, desires and unpredictability of the world-process.

EGYPTIAN BOOK OF THE DEAD
The Book of Coming Forth By Day
Dr. Muata Ashby

The ancient poet is trying to inform the open-minded reader that the age-old dilemma of the lost soul in the dream of Maya, can be resolved via true spiritual method. Very similar to that of Yoga, which is a system of spiritual 'connection' into the God-like centers inside of oneself, that initially, are so 'faraway and distant,' that the little self of the Ego cannot see into its own divine sphere. This is the situation of the young Sumerian King. As the ancient Buddhist scriptures also stated, one must cross over to the distant shore, so, with our interpretation, we can take the Sumerian poet, the Indian Yogis and the early Hinayana Buddhists as being in total agreement, even though spanning thousands of years. The Greeks also come to mind, with Pythagoras advising, around 500 BCE, to "Know the Empire of Yourself," which can be seen as another poetic expression of the Wisdom Body of humankind. The Epic predates these later spiritual systems in literature, but it is likely they exchanged views as vocalized ideas—ones that existed for thousands of years before the Vedas were finally written in 1500 BCE, millennia after the Epic of Gilgamesh. The Cosmic Flood of Maya is not to be confused with the numerous religious depictions of great physical watery deluges, or massive floods that are described in the vast majority of ancient literature. There are, however, a few sources that match well with the Epic of Gilgamesh, concerning the deluge of Maya and achieving Immortality.

In the Indus Valley civilization, the Bhagavata Purana relates the tale of an ancient Rishi named Markandeya. Rishi's are spiritual poets—they sing poems to the Gods. The Rishi, in his devout request to Vishnu, the King of Gods and Maya itself, asks to be shown the true nature of God's energetic illusion. Those under the spell of Maya are seen to be asleep, as Vishnu's illusion envelopes the entire world. After Markandeya's request to see his power of Maya, Vishnu, declaring himself to the sage as Time and Death itself, appears suddenly as an infant floating on a fig leaf in a vast infinite watery deluge. Markandeya goes into the infant's mouth to escape the surging waters. The infant swallows the Rishi, who is thus seen **as the sole survivor of the Cosmic Flood of Maya**. The sage then sees visions of various worlds of the universe, Gods and his own hermitage, while in the infant's belly. Markandeya discovered, it is said, 'all the worlds, the seven regions and the seven oceans.' Various mountains and kingdoms, along with their living inhabitants, were seen. Markandeya did not know what to make of his vision and prays to his God, as Vishnu in the form of Nara-Narayana: The Man-and-God. At that precise moment, the cosmic infant breathes out the sage, who quickly tries to embrace the infant, but everything disappears, and the sage realizes that he was in his hermitage the whole time. He was merely given a flavor of Vishnu's Maya, which can be seen as a ubiquitous, ongoing flood of illusion.

To illustrate this universal flood, let's flash forward for a quick moment. It's rather remarkable that 4,000 years later, a certain Swiss scientist named Albert Einstein declared: "Reality is an Illusion, although a very persistent one." Yes, indeed, the great dreamlike Flood of Maya is ongoing in the tick of every second of every century. Going back 50,000 years, we find the Australian ancients (aborigines) spoke first of the 'Dreamtime,' in which we find ourselves immersed, even to modern times.

In returning to Markendeya's story, the God Vishnu then appeared before the Rishi, and the Rishi stayed with him for over a thousand years, again, suggesting a Gilgamesh-like gift of immortality, after showing him the way out of the cosmic flood of illusion.

As an example of higher and lesser meanings that develop in ancient literature, it was Markandeya who wrote beautiful spiritual poems and taught about the great 'Wish Fulfilling Tree' as a true pictorial depiction of one's desires and thus one's karma. Later, over the centuries, as his spiritual ideas spread into the Hindi masses, a lesser meaning of the mystical tree developed, and people would actually make small wish-fulfilling trees, and commercially market them.

This was remarkably similar to today's religious products, where another tree—a wooden or metal one called a Christian Cross, is commonly found adorning church walls, and people's necklines. This takes place among people simultaneously, as it did in Markandeya's time, several millennia ago.

People pray to their tiny, shiny metal tree that their greatest wishes and greedy human desires come true—which is another thing entirely. Markandeya represents the higher form of human consciousness. Those who buy the little cosmic trees in the market are already, even before their purchase, magically and psychologically deluded since they quite easily accept the lesser ideal. The same is true with organized religion today.

Another early Hindu story of cosmic flood creation involves Manu, the first man, who is warned by an incarnation of the God Vishnu, of a great flood. Vishnu appeared to Manu in the form of an ever-growing fish. As a fish-avatar, Vishnu warns of an impending flood which will destroy all life, so Manu builds a boat, which the God-fish towed to a nearby mountaintop to escape the deluge.

Interestingly, in the Sumerian cuneiform texts, EA, a primary primordial God, like Vishnu, is also known to take the form of being half-man and half-fish. It is possible these stories were well known in various forms, even back in pre-historic times.

In ancient China, there are also indications of a belief in a Cosmic Flood of Maya. Like the Sumerians and early Christians, it was believed that the severe flooding along the riverbank was caused by Gods (as dragons) who were being angered by the mistakes of the people. There are a number of sources of flood myths in ancient Chinese literature. Many of them contain references to an ancient flood hero named 'Nuwa' (Noah?) who 'repairs the broken heavens after a great flood or other calamity and repopulates the world with people.'

In 700 BCE, the Chinese Shujing, or 'Book of History' describes the calamity of *'floodwaters that reach into the heavens.'* Since modern science has never found floodwaters on Earth that even remotely approach the grand scale of preposterous world deluges, we should easily conclude that these ancient tales are allegories, poetically spun by different bards and poets throughout the push and veil of time, and cultural diffusion.

It is difficult, in poring over the many lines of the Gilgamesh saga, to always know immediately when historical facts, such as a local river flooding in ancient Sumer are being presented and mixed into the difficult plot, versus the potential of the poetic double entendre, which secretly reflects an entirely different spiritual meaning. It is extremely good poetry to be able to seamlessly reflect both views, and has fooled many a scholar for over 4,000 years.

As we move along Tablet 11, we will stay interested mainly in the inner storyline, as the ancient poet spins symbolic tales of metamorphosis, immortality, purification, spiritual instructions, and magical, transcendent substances.

"After the flood had swept over, and the kingship had descended

from heaven, the kingship was in Eridu."

The Sumerian King List

Eridu, the earliest city in ancient Sumer, contained a sacred temple that was called '*The House of Cosmic Waters.*' This special name can be seen as an insight into ancient priestly views of the manifested universe. The temple was adjacent to a large pond, or swamp, which was seen as spiritually alive, and possibly a 'doorway' to the vast Underworld worlds and oceans in which the Sumerian priests believed to exist.

It is taken as true that the ancient ones used scrying, or spiritual gazing, into the waters near the temple, for, according to gurus such as Manly P Hall, the 33rd-level initiate of the Freemasons secret society, gazing into reflected or refracted light can provide, or indicate, a conscious path to other dimensions. Later, this hoary practice of scrying became a mainstay technique in ancient shamanism and other early natural spiritual systems.

Way down, below the Ocean, where I want to be, I will be.

Donovan

Beautiful dragonflies, those Kulilu birds mentioned by Gilgamesh, would surely have abounded in both the temple and the nearby watery marsh. As the butterfly represented the Psyche to the later Greeks, the Sumerian priest could have considered that Kulilu birds, or dragonflies, would also have represented the transitory nature of humans, those strange, neutrally-based creatures who psychologically molt as they go through the cycles of life, death, and the beyond. The great message here is that leaving the physical body behind is essential to spiritual growth and unseen eternity.

How to Assemble an Ark ~!~ The Preserver of Life

There is much hidden meaning in the 'Saga of the Building of the Ark' in the Epic of Gilgamesh. Below are the stanzas that Utnapishtim utters while supposedly 'building a wooden ark,' but the Epic's poet is especially clever here and is cryptically writing with a remarkable ruse of 'numeric allegory.' In a stunning surprise, we find that ~tallying~ the total references of numbers below taken from the lines beneath, may once again be indicating a cosmic cycle is being completed, rather than a wooden Ark being built.

"Pitch did the children provide while the strong

brought all that was needful.

Then on the fifth day after, I laid out the shape of my vessel,

Ten gar each was the height of her sides, in accord with her planning,

Ten gar to match was the size of her deck, and the shape of the forepart.

Did I lay down, and the same did I fashion; (aye),

six times cross-pinn'd her,

Sevenfold did I divide her... divided her inwards

Ninefold: hammer'd the caulking within her,

(and) found me a quant-pole.

All that was needful I added; the hull with six shar of bitumen

Smear'd I, and three shar of pitch did I smear on the inside; some people,

95

Bearing a vessel of grease, three shar of it brought me; and one shar

Out of this grease did I leave, which the tackling consumed, and the

boatman.

Two shar of grease stow'd away; (yea), beeves for the . . . I slaughter'd,

Each day lambs did I slay: mead, beer, oil, wine, too, the workmen

Drank as though they were water and made a great feast like the New

Year."

Forgetting the fanciful, outer storyline, we look for the poet's allegorical numeric secret. Beginning with the 5th day of construction and allowing for all construction elements mentioned as numbers, we sum them together and then subtract two for 'grease stowed away', meaning it was not used in the making of the Ark. The result is a hidden cosmic SOSS, which has never been seen before in this interpretive light.

$$5+10+10+6+7+9+6+3+3+1-2=60$$

The Hidden Cosmic SOSS-Cycle, in the Epic of Gilgamesh

S urprisingly, we have revealed the hidden and sacred numeric called 'SOSS', the Sumerian cycle of 60, which we still use today in our timekeeping of minutes and hours. As we proceed with the Epic of Gilgamesh, we will find several more 'hidden' cycles. The repeated, hidden use of SOSS and its various cycles should not be underestimated. The poet purposely placed them there, but scholars have, for over 4,000 years, overlooked such encrypted mathematical clues.

The Sumerians were the first to invent the concept of 360 degrees in a circle. In Sumerian calculations, a 'divine year' was equal to 360 human years. The implication may be that mathematical cycles are very important when it comes to building a spiritual Ark. As an example, the ancient Sumerians believed in a 'River of Souls' as an afterlife location in the Milky Way. The River was accessible by two outer gates assigned to the *outer arms of the revolving galaxy*. It was believed that reincarnation cycles followed the equinoxes associated with Sagittarius and Gemini. Only then, during the correct cycle, did souls move into heavenly and earthly positions; these gates were seen as reincarnation opportunities. The Sumerians were deeply involved with cosmic movements in the sky and saw them as cycles. Even thousands of years later, in 300 BCE, in the same evolving Akkadian, Sumerian, Babylon cultures of Mesopotamia, we find the name of the chief Babylonian priest "Berososs" can be interpreted as "Bel of SOSS," meaning 'Lord of the Cycle' or something similar. Most scholars today consider Berososs simply to mean a 'shepherd of the lord,' but the presence of SOSS in his name begs to differ.

Normally, archaeological and academic researchers focus on the watery deluge in the Epic of Gilgamesh as potentially being a partially true, yet mythical portrayal of an utterly impossible event. There are dozens of such myths, including the flood of the Bible, which are taken directly from the Epic of Gilgamesh. They are in a meaningless quandary, unless they accept the true deluge as being an allegory of the Flood of Maya. Further, as we excerpt from the Epic-specific stanzas for our alternative interpretations, we should also mention that the building of the ARK is also a likely allegory, and a spiritual one at that.

Tablet 10 of The Epic continues with the Gods speaking to Utnapishtim, yet, in reviewing through a Yogic lens, we will see these words differently this time, and find deeper meaning.

"O thou Mortal, Thou of Shurippak, a dwelling pull down,

and fashion a vessel therewith; abandon possessions,

Life do thou seek, and thy hoard disregard,

and save life; every creature Make to embark in the vessel.

The vessel, which thou art to fashion, Apt be its measure;

its beam and its length be in due correspondence,

Then, on the Deep do thou launch it."

These lines smack of more poetic double entendre. Spiritual aspirants are commonly called vessels of spirit . . . and they seek eternal life, just like the King. Abandoning hoarded possessions sounds like ancient yogic instructions to avoid attachments and materialism. Saving life, while surrounded by the Flood of Maya, may mean to pass along the hidden spiritual instructions of creating and entering into one's own vessel, which is then launched towards the Immortal Deep, found beyond the Great Flood of Maya. This is an available, alternative view. The others are to believe the possibility of a huge deluge, covering the earth, like the Christian belief, or simply to believe that the poet of Gilgamesh was purposely fostering nonsense, directed at the masses.

The following excerpted Epic stanzas, if taken as poetic spiritual metaphors, can be symbolically seen as a Yogic expression, and not just bad news from God:

98

"Shall in the night let a plentiful rainfall pour down.

Then do thou enter the vessel, and straightway shut down thy hatchway.

Came then that hour appointed, did in the night let a plentiful rainfall,

pour down. View'd I the aspect of day: to look on the day bore a horror,

Wherefore I enter'd the vessel, and straightway shutdown my hatchway."

In using the yogic method and literature from AD 400, we can find immediate similarities to these curious stanzas, even though they are separated by thousands of years. The Yoga Sutras of Patanjali are two hundred aphorisms that provide deep spiritual instruction. In the book, Patanjali advises that Yoga be practiced mainly at night, where the 'fount of heaven' will open up for the truly devoted. Note that the following Patanjali stanzas support the same idea of 'shutdown' as essential to sending the Yogin sailing on his/her nightly adventure:

Tasyapi	that too
nirodheby	shutting, closing, restraining, destroying, by cessation
sarva	all
nirodhat	checking, suppressing, destroying
nirbijah	seedless
samadh	in profound meditation.

Now, we further the connection between Patanjali and Gilgamesh by noting the meaningful commentary on these Patanjali verses, as provided by Yogic scholar, B.K.S. Iyengar;

"...as a flame is extinguished when the wood is burnt out, or as rivers lose their existence on joining the sea, all volitions and impressions of the unconscious, subconscious, conscious and superconscious mind cease to exist. All of the rivers of consciousness merge in the Ocean of the Seer."

Thus, as a Yogini develops her spiritual skills, the nighttime spiritual seeker may find the Maya of the daylight difficult to bear. The daytime is then seen as surreal, phantasmagoric, and perhaps painful to endure, as noted by the poet of the Epic:

"View'd I the aspect of day: to look on the day bore a horror."

There is a point in time, the ancient poet may be saying, where a spiritual student simply doesn't believe the nonsensical nature of Maya, which is exemplified by the light of day. The best resort to overcome Maya, and to reach the Ocean of the conscious Seer, according to Patanjali, is for the Yogini to retreat into their deeper nature. Patanjali also advised the sincere Yogic aspirant to remain awake at night, meditating on spiritual affairs, as the nighttime is the prime meditative time for success. Once the Yogini finally quiets herself, then the inner Fountain begins to flow. Finally unleased, the spiritual archetypes burst forth. In modern terms, the Yogini, in finally quieting her chattering left-brain, receives the marvelous benefits that are then extended from the rest of the Wisdom Body—and delivered to the quieted Ego—from the deeper nature of the right and rear brains acting in tandem, representing a singular entity. This cranial arrangement, of course, is what makes one 'potentially' one-third human and two-thirds God. Could this regular meditation be the secretive nightly 'rainfall' of the poet, encrypted as yet another double entendre in the Epic of Gilgamesh? The poet may be only 'feigning a deluge' for the outer storyline, which is intended for the dull masses to hear. The Epic also symbolically states:

"I enter'd the vessel, and straightway shut down my hatchway"

With this statement, we see the spiritual analogy being offered by the poet. We continue with B.K.S. Iyengar, who provides commentary on how to achieve Samadhi, the great state of endless bliss:

"As all invading thoughts are brought to an end by practice and

detachment, the soul is freed from the shackles of earthly vehicles.

100

The soul alone manifests and blazes, without form, in pristine clarity."

We can note that different poets can write of a 'nighttime rainfall' which can also be represented as 'blazes without form' . . . both expressions fully reflect the extreme intensity that the Yogin experiences in his abode of Samadhi—well beyond the world and the flood of Maya.

Unlike the Biblical deluge of 40 days, the Epic of Gilgamesh relates only *six days* of flooding, followed by a 'day of rest,' which is curiously similar to the six-day creation story of the Bible, where the gray-haired deity rested upon the seventh day. In using Sumerian math of multiplying 6 days x 60, the poet is again indicating a full-circle cycle of 360 degrees.

"Six days, a se'nnight the hurricane, deluge, and tempest continued

Sweeping the land: when the seventh day came, were quelléd the warfare,

Tempest and deluge which like to an army embattail'd were fighting.

Lull'd was the sea, all spent was the gale, assuaged was the deluge..."

It is, of course, quite possible, as archaeologists have noted, that a severe, ancient Mesopotamian storm, along with its flooding, could last for six full days before it abated on the seventh day. If so, this would provide the historic fodder for the outer storyline developed by the poet, which is entirely different, and intended solely for the masses.

Another Poetic Example, of a Larger Cosmic Cycle

While our interpretation of hidden Sumerian cycles has been focused on the smaller cyclical values of 60 and 360 seen in the Epic of Gilgamesh, the Sumerians, as they scanned the ancient skies, also believed in a recurring 432,000-year cosmological cycle. As we ask the reader to understand and believe the notion of using simple mathematical addition and multiplications functions to convey hidden, poetic meaning, consider that other poets, far from the time and space of the Epic of Gilgamesh, have been doing exactly the same thing, in using numbers and symbolic metaphors to convey their cryptic meaning.

As seen below, the Poetic Edda of the 10th century Viking culture, is an obvious example of another anonymous poet's mixed use of numbers and prose. Here is another related excerpt from the New Muse Series book, *The Vikings Secret Yoga ~ The Supreme Adventure:*

~!~

"There is an obvious link between the Poetic Edda with its cryptic, numeric references to Odin's Hall of Valhalla and the exact same numbering convention found in cultures in the East. From all that we know of ancient Mesopotamia and India, it is evident that certain numbers were supposed to give access to a **knowledge of the cosmic order;** this is as early as 3200 BCE, with the first appearance of written tablets. In addition to the decimal numeric system, these ancient folks also employed sexagesimal, (another numeric system but based upon the number **60**) as a key method of depicting cosmic time, seen through the nightly overhead movements of the starry constellations. Today, we still use base-60 numbering for our daily timekeeping needs—for seconds, minutes, and hours—but do not extend base-60 notation to include large cosmic time periods, while the ancient timekeepers did indeed do so. In 280 B.C., Berososs, the learned and wise Babylonian priest, composed a list of ten symbolic, mythological, antediluvian Kings whose ruling periods totaled 432,000 years. Joseph Campbell explains this remarkable 'epoch' connection in his *Oriental Mythology, Book III ~ Masks of God*:

"There is an exact relationship between the number of years assigned by Berososs in 280 B.C.E. and the actual sum of years of one equinoctial cycle of the Zodiac. So, that we have found this number, now in Europe in 1100 A.D., in India in 400 A.D. and in Mesopotamia in 300 B.C., with reference in each case to the measure of a cosmic Eon."

Campbell is suggesting that cultural diffusion, as yet undiscovered by anthropology, is responsible for the recurring use of the 432,000-year

102

cosmic cycle. In the cryptic Poetic Edda of Iceland, written around AD 1100, we are symbolically told about this huge cosmic cycle, as revealed in the description of Odin's heavenly warrior hall:

> *"Five hundred doors and forty there are,*
> *I ween, in Valhalla's walls;*
> *Eight hundred fighters through each door fare*
> *When to War with the Wolf They Go"*

Whatever Norse symbolism was intended by the anonymous Viking poets, it remains, as perceived by leading authorities such as Campbell, that 800 times 540 yields the cosmic eon number of 432,000. Campbell also refers to the Indus Valley's use of this epochal number:

*"Furthermore, in the Indian Mahabharata and numerous other texts of the Puranic period (400 A.D. and thereafter), the cosmic cycle of four world ages, numbers 12,000 'divine years' of 360 'human years', each of which is 4,320,000 human years; and our particular portion of that cycle, the last and worst, the so-called Kali Yuga, is exactly **one-tenth** of that sum."*

~!~

So, in consideration of the literary evidence we have discovered, we can consider several clever, ruse-spinning anonymous poets to be involved in the literature—in ancient India, Sumer, and later the 10th century AD Viking culture—and to be quite capable of spinning a cosmic yarn, brilliantly using cyclic numbers, even on clay cuneiform tablets, as the fodder for their clever symbolic prose. As we proceed with our alternative explanation of the Epic of Gilgamesh, we will find yet more cosmic, cyclical clues, secretly imbedded in prose.

Chapter 8 ~ The Immortality of Utnapishtim

He took a Face from the Ancient Gallery,

and He Walked on Down the Hall

The Doors

The Immortal One

I n returning to the Epic, and continuing on Tablet 11, we find Utnapishtim explaining to King Gilgamesh how he, once merely human, finally gained immortality. Utnapishtim is seen as the sole immortal on Earth, having transcended the great Flood of Maya.

Sooth, indeed 'twas not I of the Great Gods the secret revealéd,

But to th' Abounding in Wisdom vouchsafed I a dream, and in this wise,

He of the gods heard the secret. Deliberate, now, on his counsel'.

With these stanzas, the poet is making clever use of multiple views. In modern times, we call this writing in the first, second, and third person. When we read *'twas not I of the Great Gods the secret revealed,'* we can consider the Ego of Utnapishtim speaking, and describing a great, wise dream (neural note: the left hemisphere does not dream, while the right hemisphere is known for its dreaming capacity, in concert with the rear primordial brain).

When we read *'He of the Gods heard the secret,'* we can consider an Ego speaking in the third person concerning the wise dream and its secret.

'Deliberate now, on his counsel,' is direct advice for the left hemisphere to make a good and proper 'interpretation' of the dream, which was delivered from the Deep. With these stanzas reflecting the strong, intense dream or spiritual vision that Utnapishtim received as an experience, we see that the man is forever changed, even immortalized, in his mind. This is the ancient poet's meaning. A rare psychic, spiritual glimpse of heaven is enough of a poignant psychological event, in either ancient or modern times, so that the person's life is permanently changed. They retain the glimpse of heaven throughout their lives. As an example, let us recall the dramatic words of Pindar, the great Grecian poet of the 5th century, BCE:

> *"Creatures for a day!*
> *What is a man?*
> *What is he not?*
> *A Dream of a Shadow*
> *Is our Mortal Being.*
> *But when there comes to Men*
> *a Gleam of Splendor given of Heaven,*
> *Then rests on them a Light of Glory*
> *and Blessed are their Days."*

Psychologist Julian Jaynes made a similar neuropsychological observation in his study of Homer's classic, *The Iliad*. In his tome, *The Origin of Consciousness in the Breakdown of the Bicameral Mind*, Jaynes focuses on key human neuro-psychological developments that occurred within the past several thousand years. His use of 'the Bicameral Mind' or dual-mental-chambers, are intended to represent modern neuroscience's understanding of the brain's frontal hemispheres.

Remembering the 'conversation' that Utnapishtim has with himself, being one-third human and two-thirds God, we find Jaynes depicting the Greek King Agamemnon as also having a loud 'conversation' with his 'Gods,' who instruct the King to steal Achilles' concubine. The warrior Achilles, for his part, is enraged and wants to kill the King, but the Goddess Athena stops him. Jayne considers the possibility that Agamemnon and Achilles were hearing their left, right and rear brains in a poetical expression. In other words, they listened to their own minds, as Jaynes considers that King Agamemnon was being 'shouted at' by his internal neural deity. Below, the King explains why he was compelled to steal Achilles' beautiful, captive woman: his Gods made him do it.

"Not I was the cause of this act, but Zeus, and my portion, and the Erinyes who walk in darkness. They it was in the assembly put wild ate upon me on that day when I arbitrarily took Achilles' prize from him, so what could I do? Gods always have their way."

Jaynes portrays Achilles speaking in a similar way, with his hemispheric, internal relationship with his 'goddess of Athena.' The psychologist then summarizes his neuro-spiritual view.

*"Who then were these gods that pushed men about like robots and **sang***

***epics** through their lips? They were voices whose speech and directions*

could be as distinctly heard by the Iliadic heroes as voices are heard by

certain epileptic and schizophrenics or just as Joan of Arc heard her

106

voices. The gods were organizations of the central nervous system. The

***gods were a part of the man**, and quite consistent with this conception is*

the fact that the gods never step outside of natural laws. and can be

regarded as personae in the sense of poignant consistencies through

time, amalgams of parental or admonitory images."

After listening to Pindar and Dr. Jaynes and noting the brain-hemispheric references in ancient Grecian literature, we can return to the Epic of Gilgamesh and more completely understand. What we are saying here, is that Utnapishtim too, like King Gilgamesh, and perhaps King Agamemnon, is also one-third human and two-thirds God. The God-portion is where the great dreams and divine messages come from.

Ur-Shanabi, the cosmic boatman, is also considered in this way. In extrapolating the ancient message, we find that we are all cosmic boat-people; living, breathing vessels on a multi-dimensional sea of consciousness. We pass through many worlds, but never die.

(This is also the Author's Message to the sincere, open-minded Reader)

The following lines describing Utnapishtim's experience, are also highly symbolic and difficult to explain. The Immortal One continues to relay to Gilgamesh, that it is possible Utnapishtim is relating the details of the powerful dream which he just had or 'received' from his two-thirds God-like nature:

"Then to the Ark came up Enlil; my hand did he grasp, and uplifted

Me, even me, and my wife, too, he raised, and, bent-kneed beside me,

Made her to kneel; our foreheads he touch'd as he stood there between us,

Blessing us; 'Utnapishtim hath hitherto only been mortal,

107

Now, indeed, Utnapishtim and (also) his wife shall be equal

Like to us gods; in the distance afar at the mouth of the rivers

Utnapishtim shall dwell" So, they took me and there in the distance

Caused me to dwell at the mouth of the rivers."

We can agree with certain scholars and archaeologists that the Epic of Gilgamesh, as written, does portray a likely ancient Sumerian deluge several millennia ago . . . and that a given boat (ark) for man and animals was indeed constructed and used for Sumerian survival. The boat may have been swept out to sea for days in the Persian Gulf, but this agreement is only for the outer storyline, and doesn't employ symbolism.

Let us recall and apply Pierre Teilhard de Chardin's words:

'We are spiritual creatures having a human experience'.

It's important to see Utnapishtim in this light. He is both a spiritual being, or God-like inside, and yet, he too lived an outer, human experience, just as we, and everyone in the world, are currently doing.

In our spiritual interpretation, the outer storyline fades away, and Utnapishtim becomes the 'Ark,' as symbolic prose is used to depict a spiritual seeker necessarily becoming a vessel for a great reality. The poet chooses (and uses) the figure of Enlil, the Sumerian God of wind, air, and storms, who is said to appear in a ghostly, but non-human form. As this powerful, spiritual presence appeared to Utnapishtim in his vision, there was an overwhelming effect, which caused the 'Ego to kneel' as a symbolic gesture.

Having a God take you by the hand can be seen as more symbolic phrasing, which describes the 'connection' between the person (one-third Man) and his/her Godlike-experiences (two-thirds God). Raja Yoga also implies this connection. The Latin word 'religio' which became 'religion,' originally meant 'to bind to,' inferring a deeper self. This neuropsychological scenario is repeated throughout hundreds of pieces of ancient spiritual literature, in various forms and phrases; however, the Song Remains the Same: The little 'self' surrenders to the greater 'Self.'

Even in the Middle East, today we find the word 'Islam' to simply mean 'submission.' *Touching the Forehead* may be a symbolic gesture, for the mind's eye of humans is what is deeply impressed during a powerful spiritual vision. Although Enlil, without symbolism, is seen as a powerful God-like human figure, the inner storyline is entirely a metaphor for a shaman-like spiritual experience, when they meet with their inner, greater deity, regardless of culture. When the powerful Presence of the God is detected, Utnapishtim is psychologically lifted up—and is connected—and then absorbed into the reality of his God. His conscious-awareness greatly expanded, he lives 'before thought,' at the mouth of the rivers. He realizes this expanded state is God-like. In today's Yogic terms, we would say he is self-realized with his higher or deeper nature, as a result of his breakthrough, spiritual dream. Thus, here is the gaining of immortality for one who wakes up beyond the Flood of Maya, beyond the illusory nature of the world.

We've got nothing to hide; we're married to the same wife.

The 12 Dreams of Doctor Sardonicus, **Spirit**

In the Epic of Gilgamesh, spread over several tablets, there are several unusual references to an unnamed 'wife.' Both Utnapishtim and King Gilgamesh are spoken of as having a 'wife' but all scholars gloss over the translation without commentary, leaving the references a seeming mystery. However, a bridge of understanding can be built, but the scenario may seem a bit wild, depending upon one's tastes. Rather than omitting, or glossing over the 'wife' scenario, we will instead introduce the esteemed mythologist, Mircea Eliade. In his book, *The Mystical Marriage of a Siberian Shaman*, Eliade reports of 'spirit-wives' visiting upon the conjuring shaman, in meditation, or in strong dreams. What we are saying

109

here, is that King Gilgamesh and Utnapishtim didn't really have wives in the expected social sense. The use of 'wife' has an entirely different meaning for the Sumerian poet, who may also have been a priest in the ancient Sumerian priesthood, called 'The Gala.' The Gala priests were known for both their homosexual and heterosexual preferences; they were transvestites, incorporating both male and female aspects within themselves. The Galas had remarkable no-holds-barred sexual orgies in their temples. In his book, *The Origins and Role of Same-Sex Relations in Human Societies*, author James Neill writes:

"From earliest Sumerian times, a significant percentage of the persons

of both temples and palaces were individuals who, like the two-spirit of

the American Indians, were viewed as being neither male nor female, but

more like a third sex."

Today, with a lesser intensity, we don't use the word 'wife' but we might refer to a man getting in touch with his 'feminine' side. So, we can discard the poetic distraction of human wives; the entire reference is ancient spiritual symbolism. Another curious example of spirit-wives may be seen in the ancient biblical names of Abraham and Sarah, the patriarch and his 'wife'—more is revealed in the upcoming New Muse book *The Colors of Mind in Ancient Times*.

Now that Utnapishtim has explained to Gilgamesh how, through the life-changing spiritual dream-vision that he had, he became immortal, The Immortal One sets his wizened eyes upon the young King and expresses his concern for Gilgamesh's spiritual evolvement:

But thee, as for thee, pray, Who will assemble the gods for thy need,

that the life which thou seekest thou mayst discover?

Come, fall not asleep for six days, aye, a se'nnight!

110

Analytical, conservative scholars do not understand the spiritual implications we have developed via the development of our inner storyline. Their general consensus, in interpreting these stanzas, is that King Gilgamesh is coming to a dead end. They perceive Utnapishtim as urging the King not to fall asleep for six full days, and that he is too mortal to resist even sleep, etc., but once again we can spy the poet's ruse. In using Utnapishtim's spiritual dream as a securing anchor point for successful transcendence to immortality, we see him asking the King, "How will You do it? Who will assemble the Gods for You?" Again, the poet indicates with six days of SOSS (6x60=360) that a full cycle is complete. It does NOT mean physical sleep—that's the element of the outer storyline.

Remember: Maya is considered as sleeping consciousness by Eastern thought, and so we can interpret the sleeping advice as meaning to rise above Maya . . . to be fully conscious in your awareness for an extended period. This is truly good advice for those who can change themselves to see the world around them as an illusion, which modern theoretical physics, in its portrayal of the universe as a colossal hologram, most definitely agrees—as does the uncertainty principle of quantum mechanics. Once one knows they are in a phantasmagoric dream, then a significant turn towards deeper spiritual waters may occur, if honesty is present.

The Aborigines of Australia have been endorsing the Flood of Maya for the longest time—within their 50,000-year-old 'Dreamtime.' We can know that certain humans, perhaps only the earliest shamans or priests, truly resisted the illusion and delved deeply into the Veil of Maya . . . and what lay beyond.

As we shall see later, since King Gilgamesh's depleted mindset is not prone to visionary experiences, the Immortal One suggests Gilgamesh obtain a special magic plant which will give him immortal life. We can agree, that if one sees transcendence through life-altering experiences, with the Magic Plants being the vehicles, it is a singular, well-attested form of attaining immortality. The Magic Plant is, of course, finally revealed here as a hallucinogenic variety.

So far, we have seen two methods suggested for obtaining immortality: 1) a strong spiritual vision, 2) consciousness-affecting plants.

But there are other methods. The Yogi Patanjali, writing in his Yoga Sutras, specifies additional methods for the Yogini to achieve immortality via transcendence. The methods include: special inclination through birth and parents, prolonged fasting, prolonged meditations and prolonged postures (asanas). Patanjali also includes the use of special plants, as does Utnapishtim, for a tried-and-true way of gaining immortality.

In modern times, psychologists such as Stanislav Grof have been researching the effects of LSD and hallucinogenic plants. Grof sponsored more than 4,000 client sessions and, then, aptly, named his book *Doorway to the Numinous*, which describes the psychological gates to divine presence. In spite of the available methods, most people, however, just don't succeed in breaking through the Flood of Maya that surrounds them. In the Epic, in the character of Utnapishtim, the Sole Immortal to have survived the Flood, the poet may have been trying to indicate just how rare it is to find a true self-realized person who knows himself . . . and the Deep.

Another method of attaining immortality is discussed in Plato's *Symposium*, where Socrates, as a fledgling philosopher, travels to meet Diotima, an extremely wise woman, to learn the Art of True Love, which can bring one to a great spiritual presence. Like Utnapishtim advising King Gilgamesh on how to gain immortality, Diotima advises Socrates to seek the 'soul of beauty' and to forget the lesser, lustful moments of his youth and adulthood and to focus on the beauty of the God of Love. Diotima speaks her wisdom about Love, or Eros, to Socrates in *The Symposium*:

"And here, she said, you must follow me as closely as you can.

Socrates, there bursts upon him that wondrous vision which

is the very soul of the beauty he has toiled so long for.

It is an everlasting loveliness which neither comes nor goes, which neither flowers nor fades, for such beauty is the same on every

hand, the same then as now, here as there, this way as that way, the same

to every worshiper as it is to every other. And if, my dear Socrates,

Diotima went on, man's life is ever worth the living, it is when

he has attained this vision of the very soul of beauty. It is when he looks

upon beauty's visible presentment, and only then, that a man

will be quickened with the true, and not the seeming, virtue--for it is

virtue's self that quickens him, not virtue's semblance. And when he has

brought forth and reared this perfect virtue, he shall be called the friend

of god, **and if ever it is given to man to put on immortality, it shall be**

given to him.

After considering the strong power of love, viewed by Diotima as an 'inviolable whole,' one might speculate that Utnapishtim himself, with a great unspoken belief and love of his God, thus drew him near . . . and helped to create his spiritual vision. This method may not yet be suitable for the coarse young King of Sumer, but there are other ways, although often we have to start from scratch, as we will see in the next chapter.

Chapter 9 ~ The Leavening of Spiritual Metamorphosis

Take a pound of Love

And cook it in the Stew

Spirits of Ancient Egypt; **Paul McCartney**

I n the Epic of Gilgamesh, there are a total of three metamorphoses indicated by the poet. First, the Kulilu bird (dragonfly) is seen to transform into the Kirippu bird (the Blessed) or is at least seen as having the potential for transcendence.

Now, in the Epic's stanzas further below, the poet symbolically weaves a baking story while the King sleeps. Let us remember that in Flood of Maya, everyone is considered unawakened and sleeping. Maya, or the Great Illusion, is not simply something that ancient peoples believed in. Maya represents a great, limited truth of delusion, which may be considered as a quantum-reality flux, or a phantasmagoric view, or even a cosmic holographic illusion; these are but different words to describe the same thing: The Flood of Maya, and Maya continues to this very moment, as you read.

"Reality is an Illusion, although a very persistent one"

Albert Einstein

"Life is a Dream"

Leonard Tolstoy

While the more conservative scholarly folk would not agree, we will push on, without great technical elaboration and acknowledge, that we too, are immersed in Maya, while thinking that we are in a normal everyday 'Reality.' Modern science now speaks in terms of the universe as a hologram and/or a rather large computer simulation; these are growing theories offered by top theoretical-physicists with good mathematical support. So, it would appear to this author that we are indeed in a rather sophisticated illusion, yet the dream is still tied to our thoughts and actions, as we see with the young King. This cosmic Maya situation would include the vast majority of Gilgamesh readers, over the eons of time, including the analytical scholars who provide the recent translations for us. In researching and writing on the Epic of Gilgamesh, I have focused on numerous scholarly references. They are helpful, but it seems the ancient poet's hidden clues are always overlooked.

In the marvelous symbolic example below, which I call the Leavening of Metamorphosis, Gilgamesh sleeps while the Immortal Utnapishtim's wife bakes for six days, then, on the 7th day, the King awakens. But what is the hidden meaning? This is a scholarly head-scratcher—it seems no one knows. Fortunately, we will see an answer further below.

Then, while he sat on his haunches asleep, a breeze breathed upon

him. Spake to her, Uta-Napishtim, yea, unto his wife: "O, behold him,

E'en the strong fellow who asketh for life, how hath breathéd upon him

Sleep like a breeze!" Then his wife unto Uta-Napishtim the Distant

Answer'd: "O, touch him, and let the man wake, that the road he hath

traversed He may betake himself homeward in peace, that he by the

portal Whence he fared forth may return to his land."

Spake Uta-Napishtim, Yea, to his wife: "How the troubles of mortals do

trouble thee also!

Bake then his flour and put at his head, but the time he is sleeping

On the house-wall do thou mark it. So straightway she did so, his flour

Baked she and set at his head, but the time he was sleeping she noted

On the house-wall. So, first was collected his flour, then secondly sifted,

Thirdly, 'twas moisten'd, and fourthly she kneaded his dough, and

so fifthly Leaven she added, and sixthly 'twas baked; then seventh—he touch'd him.

All on a sudden, and so from his slumber awoke the great fellow!"

To explain the purpose of the baking, we re-introduce the related, symbolic idea of Sumerian mathematics. The primary Sumerian number was the 'SOSS' or 60, which we still use today in our timekeeping of minutes and hours. The ancient poet, in using six days of baking, soon reaches 360 degrees if we multiple by SOSS (60) . . . and thus come to a 'full circle' as we call it today. After this baking of a cosmic cycle, on the 7th day Gilgamesh was touched, or awakened.

Sumerians were the first to invent the concept of degrees-in-circle. In their times, a divine year was equal to 360 human years. By the metaphor of baking and placing the cooked loaves by Gilgamesh's head, a spiritual evolvement is being indicated—a new beginning. The King is moving; evolving from bad to good. Granted, this is not the usual scholarly viewpoint, but we must look past the mainstream academic notions, or find no meaning at all in the curious 'baking of loaves.' Many times, traditional scholars gloss over clues, and don't apparently see the ancient poet, doing his encrypting, quite brilliantly. In this author's view, the Epic of Gilgamesh is best seen as 80% poetic encrypted symbolism, and 20% probable history, which the poet uses to fashion an outer story line for the masses. No one knows for sure, of course, because the Epic is over 4,000 years old. Tablet Eleven of the Epic continues:

"Gilgamesh unto him spake, yea to Utnapishtim the Distant:

116

"Tell me, I pr'ythee , was 't thou, who when sleep was shower'd upon me

All on a sudden didst touch me, and straightway rouse me from

slumber?"

Utnapishtim to Gilgamesh spake, Yea, unto him spake he:

"Gilgamesh, told was the tale of thy meal . . . and then did I wake thee:

'One'—was collected thy flour: then 'two'—it was sifted; and 'thirdly'—

Moisten'd: and 'fourthly'—she kneaded thy dough and 'fifthly' the leaven

Added: and 'sixthly'—'twas baked: and 'seventh' —'twas I on a sudden

Touch'd thee and thou didst awake." To Uta-Napishtim, the Distant,

Gilgamesh answer'd: "O, how shall I act, or where shall I hie me,

Uta-Napishtim? A Robber from me hath ravish'd my courage,

Death in my bed-chamber broodeth, and Death is wherever I listen ."

The symbolic importance of the six steps, seen as the psychological evolution of the King, is repeated in the tale of the spiritual baking. Even today, as we read modern Yoga journals and literature, we find a similar phrasing for the spiritual development of the individual who is seeking to bring together the separate parts of their human and divine identities. First, you combine the dry ingredients—flour, sugar, salt, then stir in the water or milk. The liquids will bind the dry ingredients together. Once they are mixed, the dry and wet ingredients form a dough, which is kneaded. Then, with proper heat, the desired loaf of bread, or spiritual cake (your preference) is produced.

By placing the baked loaf, symbolic of a completed cycle, next to the King's head, the poet is psychologically signifying that the King can now potentially awake. With such a process, success might be expected . . . but Gilgamesh, after the Immortal Utnapishtim has awakened him, is still unhappy and fears death with every waking moment. As we shall see, the King still needs to be purified of his stains, in order to proceed on his quest to obtain Immortality.

Chapter 10 ~ The Purification of the King

King Gilgamesh, Hero & Tamer of Lions; courtesy Wikipedia Commons

"The first and greatest victory is to conquer yourself,

to be conquered by yourself of all things most shameful and vile."

Plato

Scholars usually interpret the hoary image above, of the Hero with his tamed, pet lion cub, to literally infer that a Sumerian King once tamed young lions, and also hunted the bigger ones, as a sign of kingship, and courage. This certainly occurred as Warrior-Kings are known to have had such interests. There is another view available, however, if we choose the symbolic route involving human psychology and the double entendre usually intended by ancient sculptors and artists.

As we see with Plato's comment, and also in many other ancient spiritual literatures, there is an ongoing, running commentary on the need for humans to conquer their core base desires, which are usually fierce, animal-like, and egotistically driven. This is also a Yogic goal of nearby India. Conquer the lesser self—the desire-driven Ego of the left-brain.

As our Sumer Hero tames his 'internal' lion, we note that the claws of the beast are placed directly over the Hero's heart and lung center, as another possible artistic inference, attaching importance to that region of the body. It's not a coincidence that Enlil, the so-called chief-God of Sumer by scholars, was also commonly known as 'Lord Breath' and granted *breath eternal*, to Utnapishtim, as he prayed. Many ancient peoples considered the sound of their own breath to be divine, and a chant-breath can be seen in the inhaling and exhaling of the divine name of Enlil. This is also known as ingressive (inhaling) and regressive (exhaling) long-vowel chanting.

Like a Yogi living thousands of years after him, Utnapishtim would have considered that simply inhaling, creates the sound of EN, and exhaling creates a sound of Lil. Thus, Enlil was called 'Lord Breath' of Sumer folk, or at least to some of the more spiritually minded ones.

(The ancient Egyptians also engaged in these breathing chant techniques, and had slightly different 'God name' sounds of their own, as revealed in an upcoming New Muse book, *The Colors of Mind in Ancient Times*.)

In the case of young Gilgamesh, with the horrible reports of his rape and enslavement of his own people, the King certainly needed to heed advice, such as that given by Plato, thousands of years later. The Song Remains the Same: The greatest challenge of men and women is to conquer their own egotistical self. Once again, we see a link to modern neuropsychology, for the Ego, as the Self-Module, resides in the left brain and lives in a constant 'feed-me' state of multiple desires, usually food, sex, power, control, etc. This is known as the brain's 'reward system' and dopamine is the primary associated neurotransmitter for this self-serving neural system. So, while we can correlate with ancient thought concerning ultra-important subjects involving life and death, it remains that they, the Sumerians, got there first, and deeply understood these neuropsychological issues, by using the reference to Gilgamesh being one-third Man (Ego) and two-thirds God (Wisdom Body). By contrast, modern analytical neuroscience is truly devoid of the knowledge of life and death, by choosing to merely map and analytically dissect the brain as their preferred method of discovery.

In many spiritual systems, there is usually a strict discipline, often accompanied by rituals, whereby an aspirant may go through the period of 'rigor' and thus rise in conscious awareness as a result. After Gilgamesh tells Utnapishtim he still fears death, the Distant One devises a plan for the King's purification or cleansing, and advises the Boatman Ur-Shanabi:

"Spake to him, yea, to the boatman Ur-Shanabi, Utnapishtim:

"'Tis thou, Ur-Shanabi . . . the crossing, will hate thee,

Sooth, to all those who come to its marge, doth its marge set a limit:

This man for whom thou wert guide—are stains to cover his body,

Or shall a skin hide the grace of his limbs? Ur-Shanabi, take him,

lead him to where he may bathe, that he wash off his stains in the water

White as the snow: let him cast off his pelts that the sea may remove

them; Fair let his body appear: of his head be the fillet renewéd,

Let him, as clothes for his nakedness, garb himself in a mantle,

Such that, or ever he come to his city, and finish his journey,

No sign of age shall the mantle betray, but preserve all its freshness."

Wherefore Ur-Shanabi took him, and where he might bathe did he lead him, washing his stains in the water like snow, his pelts, too, discarding,

So that the sea might bear them away; and his body appeared fair.

Of his head he the fillet renewed, and himself in a mantle

Garb'd, as the clothes for his nakedness, such that or ever his city

Reach he, or ever he finish his journey, the mantle betray not

Age, but preserve all its freshness. So, into their vessel embarked

Gilgamesh, aye, and Ur-Shanabi, launching their craft on the billow.

They themselves riding aboard her."

While the outer storyline simply infers the King should take a bath on the beach, the inner saga reveals symbolically that Gilgamesh, having committed great sins of lust and carnage in his youth, now rejects those actions and must shed his sins, as pelts, into the cosmic sea. Thus, there is a chance for true body and soul restoration by 'coming clean,' as we say today. By the recognition of one's guilts and errors, a person's face can gain a new countenance, as the dark shadows of the turbulent past fade away.

> *Take me to the river*
> *Wash me down*
> *Won't you cleanse my soul*
> **Bruce Springsteen**

Chapter 11 ~ The Magic Plant and the Inner Child

I wrapped my fear around me like a blanket

I sailed my ship of safety till I sank it.

Closer to Fine, **The Indigo Girls**

Y es, thus far, the darkness of the life of King Gilgamesh can be summed up in a few modern lyrics. In the Epic of Gilgamesh, scholars usually don't have elaborate comments concerning these upcoming stanzas further below, and the notion of deep spiritual meaning appears lost upon most academic researchers. However, if we continue to look openly for symbolic ideas, we will find a truly rich, age-old spiritual idea being poetically expressed. We have already noted that Utnapishtim, upon meeting the King, declared Gilgamesh to be God-like, yet apparently uninformed as to his deeper nature; further, the Immortal Distant One said upon first seeing the King—'he has no sails.' These psychic sails are not yet available to the young King, and he is forced to 'pole his way' through life, not soaring, as a King should.

The next scene of the Epic unfolds as the unknown, unnamed, perhaps spiritual 'wife' of Utnapishtim speaks, knowing the weary King is desperate to find immortal life, while having no sails. She makes a poignant suggestion to her immortal mate to help the King in his quest, since he is symbolically reduced to merely rowing through life by the seashore. The Epic continues:

To Utnapishtim, the Distant, Spake then his wife:

"Came Gilgamesh hither, a weary with rowing,

What wilt thou give wherewith he return to his land?"

and the meanwhile, Gilgamesh, lifting his pole,

was pushing the boat at the seashore.

Then answer'd Uta-Napishtim to him, yea, to Gilgamesh spake he:

"Gilgamesh, hither didst come all aweary with rowing; O, tell me,

What shall I give thee as gift wherewith to return to thy country?

*Gilgamesh, I will reveal thee **a hidden matter** . . . I'll tell thee:*

*There is a **plant** like a thorn with its root deep down in the ocean,*

Like unto those of the briar, in sooth its prickles will scratch thee,

Yet if thy hand reach this plant, thou'lt surely find life everlasting."

As we will see in subsequent stanzas, the naming of this plant has been mysterious, with interpretations yielding 'The Plant of Wonder' and also 'The Plant of Heartbeat.' Both names have important meanings, as we shall see, for a mourning, forlorn King. The symbolic reference of the plant being rooted in the bottom of the ocean is entirely symbolic.

This Ocean is the deep sea of Maya, similar in notion to the idea of the Great Flood as an expression of Maya. The ancient poets reuse the symbolism of water in various ways. The 'Source of the streams' is another water reference, with the 'Source' being beyond Maya. Taking the poetical phrases literally is like chasing fool's gold—nothing meaningful ever comes from it. After hearing Utnapishtim inform him that there is truly a chance at immortal life, Gilgamesh reacts:

Then, when Gilgamesh heard this, he loosen'd his girdle about him,

Bound heavy stones on his feet, which dragg'd him down to the sea-

deeps, found he the plant; as he seized on the plant, lo, its prickles did

scratch him. Cut he the heavy stones from his feet that again it restore

124

him unto its shore.

After hearing of the possibility of eternal life from the great Utnapishtim, the 'Distant One,' Gilgamesh is ecstatic, and the 'loosening' of the girdle may refer to a psychological relaxing, where he leaves his forlorn thoughts of death behind him. His depression leaves him, as he begins to embark on a spiritual journey, which will be activated by 'seizing' the Plant of Immortality.

These poetic, encrypted passages are especially difficult to symbolically interpret and usually leave most conservative scholars perplexed. The difficulty is resolved if we can take the significant step of considering the all-important life-giving plant to be a *psychoactive* variety. Also, based on their standard interpretation, most scholars don't consider that Gilgamesh ever actually 'ate the plant,' but we shall disagree; there is too much hidden, rich, and revealing information. Our alternative symbolic interpretation considers that the King did indeed consume the psychoactive plant after he found it, and the plant gave him greatly expanded consciousness, and carried him beyond the deep illusion of Maya, into an oceanic consciousness where the 'plant has its roots.'

This process may be referred to as 'seizing' and 'getting scratched,' or becoming entranced, or extremely high, while having slight *bodily effects*, which are expected with opiates and hallucinogenic substances, such as today's potent Ayahuasca, or psilocybin mushrooms.

> *"Direct not thy mind to the vast measures of the earth.*
>
> *For the plant of truth is not upon ground."*

Chaldean Oracles of Zoroaster

The curious stanzas of binding and cutting stones from the feet must not be taken literally, as we don't think Gilgamesh actually jumped into the sea with stones on his feet to go to the bottom of the watery ocean. The author of the Epic may be trying to poetically infer that we are bound by psychological stones to a certain level of consciousness. Another possibility might be related to the modern axiom of 'Keeping One's Feet on the Ground, while having One's Head in the Clouds', by being transcendent. Around 500 BCE, Siddhartha Gotama, the Hinayana Buddha, once informed his monks that 'any monk that rises up and looks down upon his body . . . will never die.'

The use of the sacred plant provides the key—the message of immortality. David O. Kennedy, author of *Plants and the Human Brain* notes:

"The first unequivocal, written evidence of mankind's enduring

relationship with psycho-tropic plants is provided by clay tablets bearing

the 'cuneiform' script. These clay tablets originated in the Sumerian

civilization that flourished from the 4th to 1st millennia BC in

Mesopotamia. The tablets, dated to the middle part of the 3rd millennium

BC, record the use of some 250 plants, including the opium poppy,

mandrake, and deadly nightshade."

Yet another translation of the magic plant renders "How-the-Old-Man-Once-Again-Becomes-a-Young-Man." The Sumerians, with their large psychoactive pharmacopoeia, also wrote of a special plant called HU-GIL,' or 'plant of joy.' Could such a magic plant have contributed to the very naming of the King? Consider GIL-GA-MESH, as 'He Who Saw the Deep.'

Nearby Egypt and India also were known for their use of such plants, some of which were difficult to handle, such as the prickly opium plant. The Egyptian concoction may have created a transcendent, extremely colorful experience called 'The Green Eye of Horus.' The Hindu Soma drink, a psychedelic plant mixture now long lost and forgotten, was considered a vehicle for ecstatic departures into the expanded regions well beyond the ordinary mind. The Egyptians and Sumerians especially favored psychoactive mushrooms and the hallucinogenic blue water lily. It is

126

possible, that the blue water lily, properly consumed via mixture and proper ritual, may be the magic plant mentioned in the Epic, as the early priests consumed them for the same purpose as Gilgamesh—to get connected to our deeper nature, which is eternal. Our position concerning the relation of divinity and the special magic plant is strengthened by David Kennedy's view, where he speaks of the ancient Egyptians and their belief:

"The hallucinogenic experience of consuming these mushrooms was

believed to confer immortality and divinity to the consumer and allow

direct communication with the gods."

We can infer that the ancient Sumerian poet also believed the same and encrypted the spiritual message into the inner storyline of the Epic of Gilgamesh, deceiving many an academic scholar. One has to be careful with consciousness-affecting plants such as Ayahuasca, because the heartbeat is indeed increased. One could very easily describe Ayahuasca or even the magic mushrooms, as Plants of Wonder or Plants of Heartbeat, which are both names for the King's plant. Let's remember that Gilgamesh, 'He Who Saw the Deep,' was in deep painful remorse and emotionally desperate when he first encountered the Immortal 'Distant One' Utnapishtim. Even though we speak of ancient cultures in Egypt, Sumer and India, the effects of these same psychoactive plants are still seen several thousand years later, in our own societies.

While Gilgamesh was terrified of death 4,000 years ago, the same terror remains true today for many people. It's important to note that in modern social psychology, a 'Terror Management' theory has been developed, where everyday people, depressed and disconnected from the failed religious systems of their society, experience what is psychologically referred to as a 'self-preservation' conflict. Like the ancient King, they become scared to Death . . . of Death. They don't believe in the afterlife as expressed by any particular religious system and become psychologically impacted and terrified at the specter of death. The psychological premise is the same as ancient Gilgamesh.

Remarkably, here in Colorado, these plants are now, once again, fully legal. In full resonance with the ancient story of experiencing divinity via psychoactive plants, researchers have found that terrified patients, after taking a prescribed psychoactive substance, *lose all fear of death*; such is the immense strength of the plant, or mushroom. They become like Gilgamesh: *'He Who Saw the Deep.'* They transcend the Ego and the normal view of Earth life. Utnapishtim was right, glimpses of one's own immortality can be experienced by magical plants. This is still true today, but the intensity of the experience is compelling, and not for the faint-hearted.

American movie celebrity Lindsey Lohan, who experienced an intense Ayahuasca session with her friends, spoke afterwards of going through a deep, emotional Ego-death, before being intensely reborn into a totally new spiritual person. Thus, the great, intense message of the transcendent plants has echoed throughout the great millennia; they restore a youthful vitality to the human creature who ingests it. In a way, they become forever-new, like their inner child has been reborn. The ancient Sumerian and Egyptian artists used dragonflies (the Kulilu bird) and butterflies as their creative metaphors for the metamorphosis of change seen in life and death.

Sumerian scholar Alfred Jeremias, summarized the earliest spiritual belief, which is over 4,000 years old:

> *"Man is a spiritual being;*
>
> *an image of divinity veiled in earthly clothing."*

The ancient song of truth remains the same, with Pierre Teilhard de

Chardin, writing in our twentieth century:

> *"We are spiritual beings having a human experience"*

Even modern rock groups, like Sting and The Police, report the ancient message, via lyrics such as:

> *We are Spirits, in the Material World.*

Before consuming the psychoactive plant, Gilgamesh is impressed and convinced of its mind-altering properties, and says so to his cosmic boatman, Ur-Shanabi, before they journey back to the King's home city of Erech (Uruk). The King plans on giving the sacred plants to others. .

Gilgamesh spake to him, yea, to the boatman Ur-Shanabi, this wise:

"Nay, but this plant is a plant of great wonder, Ur-Shanabi," said he,

"Whereby a man may attain his desire—I'll take it to Erech,

Erech, the high-wall'd, and give it to eat unto

'Greybeard-who-turneth-to-man-in-his-prime' is its name and I'll eat it

I myself, that again I may come to my youthful condition."

The 'youthful condition' refers to the inner psychology or the 'inner child' of the King—not the physical body, which will die, as the inner King lives on. The Epic of Gilgamesh is only one of hundreds or thousands of pieces of literature that refer to ancient humans accessing a youthful mindset and divinity through psychoactive plants. The book *The Plants of the Gods ~ Their Sacred, Healing and Hallucinogenic Powers* by Schultes, Hofmann and Ratsch, provides an excellent insight on this ancient, still-essential practice of using magical plants.

Chapter 12 ~ The Mystery of the Snake

Ride the snake, ride the snake, to the lake, the ancient lake.

The Doors.

T he story of the Snake in the Epic of Gilgamesh is one of the most misunderstood segments of the entire saga of the Ancient King. The shrewd poet of Sumer, going into symbolic and hallucinogenic areas not normally observed by the conservative, academic scholar, weaves a day-in-the-life story of what it means to psychologically rise and fall from great spiritual heights, which were encountered and brought on by the ingestion of the sacred psychoactive plant.

Among the many interpretations of the name 'Utnapishtim,' we find several that render as 'Day of Life' or 'A Day in the Life,' which suggests a temporal meaning behind the designation of Life itself.

As seen below, the mainstream version of this ancient story is far too simple: Gilgamesh takes a bath and a mysterious snake darts up from the lake depths, and suddenly steals his magic plant, and the King weeps at his great misfortune. Thus, the Epic once again appears to resemble childish gibberish in the outer storyline, but let's take a deeper look through our alternative symbolic lens, provided below, after the Epic's stanzas of the Snake.

Broke they their fast at the fortieth hour: at the sixtieth rested.

Gilgamesh spied out a pool of cool water, and therein descending

Bathed in the water. But here was a serpent who snuff'd the plant's

fragrance, darted he up from the water, and snatch'd the plant, uttering

malison, as he drew back. Then Gilgamesh sate him and burst into weeping. Over his cheeks flow'd his tears: to the boatman Ur-Shanabi

spake he, "Pr'ythee, for whom have toiléd mine arms, O Ur-Shanabi, tell

me, Pr'ythee, for whom hath my heart's blood been spent?

Yea, not for mine own self.

Have I the guerdon achieved; no, 'tis for an earth-lion only.

Have I the guerdon secured; and now at the fortieth hour?

Such an one reiveth it; O, when I open'd the sluice and the

attachment, Aye, I noted the sign which to me was vouchsafed as a

warning, Would I had turn'd and abandon'd the boat at the marge of the

ocean!"

As mentioned earlier, our alternative interpretation differs from the mainstream scholarly view, in that they consider that the King never eats the plant but loses it. Our view is that the King does indeed consume the magic plant, but as we shall see, it only provides a 'temporary' ladder to the desired God-like state; the 'mouth of the river' as the sole immortal, Utnapishtim called it.

In our interpretation, the poet begins the story of the serpent with a line about fasting and resting; once again we have the mysterious numeric elements of 40 and 60 being presented, with 60 being a 'full SOSS.' This is another poetic exposure to the fraction of two-thirds.

In an alternative view, after consuming the plant, King Gilgamesh is still in a God-like connection with the upper regions of conscious awareness, due to its effects. He sees a cool lake and decides to lie down in it, which has an immediate chilling effect on his body. The ancient symbolism of the lake water and snake symbolism is extremely important, as Joseph Campbell points out in his book *The Mythic Image*:

'The reptile is symbolic of the primal generative waters that surround the universe...the fluency of the serpent suggests...water'.

While the Sumerians and many ancient cultures believed in a cosmic serpent, this idea was localized to the bodies of water near or in Sumerian cities. We are saying here, that, in a spiritual sense, to the ancient Sumerian scribe, the snake IS the spirit of the water. In the ancient city of Eridu, the Sumerian priests craft consecrated and revered certain, local pools of water; they considered it divinely alive and kept a small portion of the pool water in sacred containers for use in temple rituals. In following this ancient belief, in our poetical interpretation, we suggest that the ancient scribe is using the cold lake water, as representing the spirit of the 'snake' or serpent, in the inner storyline of the Epic:

"But here was a serpent who snuff'd the plant's fragrance,

Darted he up from the water, and snatch'd the plant, uttering malison,

As he drew back."

The interpretation of 'snuffing of the plants fragrance' is a wily poet's phrase. It is well known amongst drug therapists that cold water is often used as a bathing technique of bringing an overdosed person down from their 'high.' Let's consider that Gilgamesh entered the water while connected to the God-like state via the plant, and after a few short moments, found that he was 'disconnecting' from that vast state . . . and it was the water that was having a chilling effect on his extended state of consciousness. In this scenario, we see the King darting up from the cool water, no longer God-like in consciousness, and grabbing a plant and cursing it (uttering malison), for its temporary, illusive nature. The words "As he drew back" indicate a distinct and abrupt change in the King's awareness: he was coming down from his God-like high. The followers of the outer storyline think that a snake actually stole the plant, perhaps, in

132

some strange way, to gain its own immortality. Further, some interpretations of the Epic mention that the snake 'shed its skin as it was departing,' but perhaps this is a poetic metaphor for the King to shed his shallow, egotistical nature as well. Whosoever does so, becomes unencumbered, and moves towards their own immortality. In addition to the symbolic relation of the serpent to the depths of the water, the snake is also considered an emblem for wisdom, knowledge, and danger, for the Ego is always afraid of the greater depth of consciousness, which is yet housed in the human Wisdom Body.

In this sense, we, as Ego, are one-third human and the remaining Wisdom Body of our right and rear brains and our neural Heart and its neural blood represent our deeper nature of being 'two-thirds God-like.' As stated earlier, our right and rear brains have extended neural arms with which they can communicate; together, this represents a potentially greater Self than the left-brain Ego, yet our human self must decide the nature of reality.

Gilgamesh, after all of his and Ur-Shanabi's strong efforts, seems extremely disappointed, once again. The King was once connected to the expansive God-like state via the properties of the magic plant and had soared to marvelous heights of consciousness.

He breaks down and cries at his re-entry into the death-prone human state, once again. The 'guerdon' or reward seems to the King to be only for a strong lion, such as himself, to be bound to the Earth, again awaiting death, at the fortieth hour, perhaps two-thirds of the way into the journey of life, with the shorter Sumerian life expectancy.

Today, we might call this a severe psychological mid-life crisis. The ancient poet may be insinuating that the God-like state may be fleeting, and unsustainable for one such as the spiritually seeking, yet undeveloped King. We revisit a few lines from the Epic below, with Gilgamesh speaking:

Such an one reiveth it; O, when I open'd the sluice .

133

(Aye), I noted the sign which to me was vouchsafed as a warning,

Would I had turn'd and abandon'd the boat at the marge (of the ocean)!'

These cryptic passages are difficult, as the poet seems to be saying that one can be revived when they open the 'sluice.' The word sluice can be seen as activating a conscious 'channel,' which is a good description for an expansive psychoactive experience. Sensing a psychic warning, the King considers turning and abandoning himself (the boat) at the edge of the extremely expansive ocean of primordial, undifferentiated conscious-awareness, as an expression of a death wish. The poet may be indicating that, after such a tremendous oceanic experience in the extended states, one may not want to come back to Earth again, with its painful ways . . . and Death. But the effects of the plant have worn off and once again, the King is in the Flood of Maya. Gilgamesh has, however, learned of the greater consciousness beyond the ordinary, meaningless life, and has gained key spiritual experience as a result of his encountering Utnapishtim and the Magic Plant.

In this scenario, we might infer that Utnapishtim *knew* of the plant's consciousness-affecting magic, because he had already experienced the Plant, and its gift of immortality. The poet may be trying, through the vehicle of the King, to indicate that some people don't really trust their own deep psychic and spiritual experiences after they've had them, as they return to everyday life. That's the nature of the insecure Ego, which may hesitate to try to attain such vast, God-like states again. Thus, the boat would stay in the small harbor of its illusion and not the vast ocean, which remains forever available . . . but at a considerable, faraway distance.

Thousands of years later, beginning in 1927, psychologists Sigmund Freud, Carl Jung, et al, studied patients who reported an 'oceanic' experience of consciousness or of being one-with-the-universe. Freud considered that the oceanic experience, if it existed, was an infantile pre-Egoic expression, and that it fostered the fantastic emotive energy that expresses and breaks down into the various religious systems. This seems a degraded view, in this author's opinion. Freud and Jung were themselves extremely interested in having such an experience, but it eluded them, because analytical psychology is not the vehicle for such psychological releases. Plus, cocaine, Freud's drug of choice, does not yield such expansive hallucinogenic experiences. After thinking of the four millennia that have passed between the writing of Gilgamesh and the observations by Freud and Jung, we might expect the experience of the Great Ocean of conscious-awareness to be a sacred one, likely going deep back into the pre-historic, Neolithic times.

The poet seems to indicate that the immortal Utnapishtim, the Faraway One, is more psychically established than Gilgamesh, in maintaining the conscious 'channel' or 'sluice' to the great 'Mouth of the Rivers,' where Utnapishtim has his eternal home, in God-like conscious awareness.

Chapter 13 ~ The Pride of the Architect: The Ego rises

All we do crumbles to the ground though we refuse to see.

Dust in the Wind; **Kansas**

After Gilgamesh's great psychic disappointment at having fallen from the ladder to the Gods, indeed, from the heights of immortality, the poet sets the stage for the final scene of the Epic. The King, accompanied by Ur-Shanabi, his boatman, start the journey back to Gilgamesh's hometown of Erech (Uruk).

Broke they their fast at the fortieth hour: at the sixtieth rested,

So, in the end to the middle of Erech, the high-wall'd, arrivéd.

Gilgamesh spake to him, yea, to the boatman Ur-Shanabi this wise:

"Do thou, Ur-Shanabi, go up and walk on the ramparts of Erech,

Look on its base, and take heed of its bricks, if its bricks be not kiln-

burnt, Aye, and its ground-work be not bitumen, e'en seven courses,

One shar the city, and one shar the gardens, and one shar the

. . . .the Temple of Ishtar, amass'd I three shar, of Erech.

Thus, concludes the Epic of Gilgamesh. The poet again announces the partial SOSS cycle of two-thirds, with his stanza concerning fasting and resting. Most scholars consider that King Gilgamesh, in these final stanzas of Tablet 11 (The Flood), is signifying his human 'immortality' through lasting, memorable deeds performed at his home city of Erech. Hence, this section is often called 'the Pride of the Architect.' The poet could be suggesting that Gilgamesh, as a human Ego only, will have his kingly name immortalized in history, thus a type of immortality is achieved. Yet the conclusion is almost tongue-in-cheek, after consideration of the numerous entries previously observed in our inner-sanctum storyline. The very last stanza indicates where a few undecipherable breaks occurred in the ancient cuneiform copy and this is noteworthy. There are hundreds of such cuneiform breaks in the Epic's eleven tablets. Archaeologists and linguistic scholars have done a remarkable job in restoring what little information we have. Much of the 'standard' version of the Epic of Gilgamesh has been necessarily re-assembled from the versions found in ancient Akkadian, Sumerian, and Babylonian temples and libraries. While our last interpretation of the Epic has focused on Tablet 11, we also know, from the other tablets, that the King was, in his youth, a horrible tyrant who raped betrothed women and set young male children upon the walls of Erech, basically becoming his slaves. The people were repressed. So, it is with this backdrop that we should consider the 'immortality of youth,' as stated by author Somerset Maugham, to reflect the lesser path of the youthful King, when he was pure, unrestrained Ego, emotionally immature, and incapable of understanding the nature of death.

Conclusions

In concluding this brief, alternative commentary to a marvelous 4,000-year-old poem, let us finish on the key theme of Body, Mind & Spirit as stated initially in the introduction. Thus, the image of the dragonfly, or Sumerian Kirippu bird, represents the ascending immortal, molting spirit, and the images of King Gilgamesh and Enkidu, that of the mortal predicament, the Kulilu bird, pertaining to the body. But let us remember that King Gilgamesh, and also red-furred Enkidu, and everyone who has ever lived, all have had this Kirippu-Transcendence of, or spirit of flight, inside of them, which is finally released at death of the body.

~!~

We are all one-third human and two-thirds divine.

Understanding our Wisdom Body can be easily described as Knowing Oneself, as Socrates advised, or in the Yogic symbol of AUM, the universal self, which accurately describes the three cranial brains in the human skull, and the ever-pulsing neural heart. These are the important aspects of the total human Wisdom Body, which can be considered in its known neural, electromagnetic, chemical, and cellular aspects. Taken together, these elements create the vital, dynamic conduit to our deeper nature, and immortality. We have but to assemble them, yogically integrate them, and upon doing so, will create our own spiritual Path.

In spite of the many broken tablets and the unimpressive ambiguous ending in the final tablet, there are several conclusions that can serve as lessons. Firstly, although I have enjoyed writing this alternative commentary, I certainly acknowledge that it remains incomplete, while also acknowledging that a certain, new spiritual light has been shown on the ancient text. It is highly unlikely that anyone will fully decipher the Epic of Gilgamesh, with its many poetic twists and turns and broken clay scratchings. Hopefully, however, the open-minded reader will agree with this author, that there is a remarkable, hidden, spiritual underpinning to the Epic of Gilgamesh, and that it is poetically encrypted in many ways. Moreover, in the total counting of the many thousands of recovered ancient Sumerian tablets, the Epic of Gilgamesh is only 11–12 tablets in its entirety. There are dozens of other legends and writings concerning the ancient King, many of which conflict and/or introduce new elements, as might be expected over the eons of time. Long after his death, Mesopotamian people worshipped Gilgamesh. He was first renowned as a warrior and builder and then was widely celebrated for his wisdom and judiciousness. One prayer even invokes him as "Gilgamesh, supreme King, judge of the Anunnaki" (the Gods of the Underworld, in this context).

In the very earliest texts, the King is referred to as 'Bil-ga-mes,' which translates as *'the divine old ancestor who became young.'* This suggests that the King really did succeed in his quest for immortality. Anyone spiritually successful will recognize an ancient wisdom here, pointing to our precocious Inner Child and even deeper levels of awareness.

One of the earliest shamanistic, *panpsychic* beliefs is that an ancient, primordial creature, which many would call God in modern times, is actually expressing itself through the human vehicle.

Thus, the unknown Sumerian Scribe penned the details of the King's very life, as seen through the lens of the expression, of this primordial consciousness.

Yet, as seen in the rare Utnapishtim, and perhaps a wiser Gilgamesh, there are very few souls that truly escape Maya, the hanging gardens of this amazing dream world, while alive. To awake is always staggering and the cosmic cycles of awakening are endlessly ongoing. So, we are all travelers on this, the ancient, now modern, universal path to our own Immortality.

You're never gonna die, You're gonna make it if you try.

Pink Floyd

"No One Ever Dies"

Steven A Key

'TIS THE END

Appendix A ~ The Sacred Texts

Many thanks to the good folks at Sacred-Texts.com for their help.

The entire Epic of Gilgamesh can be found online at the following site:

http://www.sacred-texts.com/ane/eog/index.htm

Appendix B ~ The Preface ~ By R. Campbell Thompson

While this provocative book examined and explained many new mysterious elements found in the 4,000-year-old Epic of Gilgamesh, it remains that we touched upon only a fraction of the Epic's total lines of script. It may be helpful to the reader, for contrast, to understand a more standardized view, that of R. Campbell Thompson, a major translator of the original twelve cuneiform tablets. Here is his Preface to the Epic of Gilgamesh, which explained his translation in 1927.

Preface to The Epic of Gilgamesh

"The Epic of Gilgamesh, written in cuneiform on Assyrian and Babylonian clay tablets, is one of the most interesting poems in the world. It is of great antiquity, and, inasmuch as a fragment of a Sumerian Deluge text is extant, it would appear to have had its origin with the Sumerians at a remote period, perhaps the fourth millennium, or even earlier. Three tablets of it exist written in Semitic (Akkadian), which cannot be much later than 2,000 B.C.: half a millennium later come the remains of editions from Boghaz Keui, the Hittite capital in the heart of Asia Minor, written not only in Akkadian, but also in Hittite and another dialect. After these comes the tablet found at Ashur, the old Assyrian capital, which is anterior in date to the great editions now preserved in the British Museum, which were made in the seventh century B.C., for the Royal Library at Nineveh, one Sin-liqi-unni(n)ni being one of the editors. Finally, there are small neo-Babylonian fragments representing still later editions.

In the seventh century edition, which forms the main base of our knowledge of the poem, it was divided into twelve tablets, each containing about three hundred lines in meter. Its subject was the Legend of Gilgamesh, a composite story made up probably of different myths which had grown up at various times round the hero's name. He was one of the earliest Kings of Erech in the South of Babylonia, and his name is found written on a tablet giving the rulers of Erech, following in order after that of Tammuz (the God of vegetation and one of the husbands of Ishtar) who in his turn follows Lugal-banda, the tutelary God of the House of Gilgamesh. The mother of Gilgamesh was Nin-sun. According to the Epic, long ago in the old days of Babylonia (perhaps 5,000 B.C.), when all the cities had their own Kings, and each state rose and fell according to the ability of its ruler, Gilgamesh is holding Erech in thrall, and the inhabitants appeal to the Gods to be relieved from his tyranny. To aid them, the wild man Enkidu is created, and he, seduced by the wiles of one of the dancing girls of the Temple of Ishtar, is enticed into the great city, where at once (it would appear) by ancient right Gilgamesh attempts to rob him of his love. A tremendous fight ensues, and mutual admiration of each other's prowess follows, to so great an extent that the two heroes become firm friends, and determine to make an expedition together to the Forest of Cedars which is guarded by an Ogre, Humbaba, to carry off the cedar wood for the adornment of the city. They encounter Humbaba, and by the help of the Sun-God who sends the winds to their aid, capture him and cut off his head; and then, with this exploit, the goddess Ishtar, letting her eye rest on the handsome Gilgamesh, falls in love with him. But he rebuffs her proposal to wed him with contumely, and she, indignant at the insult, begs her father Anu to make a divine bull to destroy the two heroes. This bull, capable of killing three hundred men at one blast of his fiery breath, is overcome by Enkidu, who thus incurs the punishment of hubris at the hands of the Gods, who decide that, although Gilgamesh may be spared, Enkidu must die. With the death of his friend, Gilgamesh in horror at the thought of similar extinction goes in search of eternal life, and after much adventuring, meets first with Siduri, a goddess who makes wine, whose philosophy of life, as she gives it him, however sensible, is evidently intended to smack of the hedonism of the bacchante. Then he meets with Ur-Shanabi (the boatman of Uta-Napishtim) who may perhaps have been introduced as a second philosopher to give his advice to the hero, which is now lost; conceivably he has been brought into the story because of the

143

sails(?) which would have carried them over the Waters of Death (by means of the winds, the Breath of Life?), if Gilgamesh had not previously destroyed them with his own hand. Finally comes the meeting with Uta-Napishtim (Noah) who tells Gilgamesh the story of the Flood, and how the Gods gave him, the one man saved, the gift of eternal life. But who can do this for Gilgamesh, who is so human as to be overcome by sleep? No, all Uta-Napishtim can do is to tell him of a plant at the bottom of the sea which will make him young again, and to obtain this plant Gilgamesh, tying stones on his feet in the manner of Bahrein pearl-divers, dives into the water. Successful, he sets off home with his plant, but, while he is washing at a chance pool, a snake snatches it from him, and he is again frustrated of his quest, and nothing now is left him save to seek a way of summoning Enkidu back from Hades, which he tries to do by transgressing every taboo known to those who mourn for the dead. Ultimately, at the bidding of the God of the Underworld Enkidu comes forth and pictures the sad fate of the dead in the Underworld to his friend: and on this somber note the tragedy ends.

Of the poetic beauty of the Epic there is no need to speak. Expressed in a language which has perhaps the simplicity, not devoid of cumbrousness, of Hebrew rather than the flexibility of Greek, it can nevertheless describe the whole range of human emotions in the aptest language, from the love of a mother for her son to the fear of death in the primitive mind of one who has just seen his friend die; or from the anger of a woman scorned to the humour of an editor laughing in his sleeve at the ignorance of a savage. Whether there is justification for taking the risk of turning it into ponderous English hexameter meter is an open question, but in so doing I have done my utmost to preserve an absolutely literal translation, duly enclosing in a round bracket, (), every amplification of the original phrasing which either sense or meter or particularly an appreciation of unproven Assyrian particles has demanded. Restorations, either probable from the context or certain from parallels, have been enclosed in square brackets [].

To George Smith, one of the greatest geniuses Assyriology has produced, science owes much for the first arrangement and translations of the text of

144

this extraordinary poem: indeed, it was for this Epic that he sacrificed his life, for actually it was the discovery of the Deluge Tablet in the British Museum Collections which led the Daily Telegraph to subscribe so generously for the re-opening of the diggings in the hope of further finds at Kouyunjik (Nineveh), in conducting which he died all too early in 1876. Sir Henry Rawlinson and Professor Pinches played no small part in the reconstruction and publication of at least two of the tablets, and to their labours in this field must be added the ingenuity of Professor Sayce, and the solid acumen of Dr. L. W. King. In America to Professor Haupt is owed the first complete edition of the texts, very accurately copied, and later on the editions of two early Babylonian texts were edited by Langdon, Clay and Jastrow: among German publications must be mentioned the translations of Jensen and Ungnad, with the edition of an Old Babylonian tablet by Meissner. The Boghaz Keui texts have been edited by Weidner, Friedrich, and Ungnad. It would be superfluous to say how much I am indebted to the labours of all these scholars.

The present version is based on a fresh collation of the original tablets in the British Museum, the results of which I propose to publish shortly in a critical edition of both text and translation. It will be seen that I have departed from the accepted order of several of the fragments of which the position in the Epic is problematical. An examination of numerous fragments of tablets of a religious nature has naturally led to the discovery of duplicates and joins, some of which will be apparent in the present text. For their great liberality in granting me facilities to copy and collate these valuable tablets I have to express my heartiest thanks to the Trustees of the British Museum, and the Director, Sir Frederick Kenyon. To my friends Dr. H. R. Hall, and Messrs. Sidney Smith and C. J. Gadd of the British Museum, I am greatly indebted for much help in forwarding the work: and to Sir John Miles, Fellow of Merton College, Oxford, I owe many shrewd suggestions."

R. CAMPBELL THOMPSON. NINEVEH, CHRISTMAS, 1927.

Appendix C ~ Speaking with the Gods

This appendix is for those eBook readers who chose to read the entire Epic via the weblink provided in Appendix A, or those who are already intimately familiar with the Epic of Gilgamesh.

In this writing, I deleted certain duplicated stanzas of the Epic, for easier understanding.

However, the astute reader may have noticed that many lines in the whole version of the Epic of Gilgamesh appear needlessly duplicated, however this is not the case, nor a repeated scribal error.

In 1944, Sumerian mythology researcher Samuel Noah Kramer, noted for the first time, the reason that several of the Epic's stanzas appear needlessly duplicated, when one stanza occasionally repeats the other. Academic understanding was stumped, until Kramer, one of the foremost scholars of his time, finally found the answer, as he reveals below:

"The Sumerian poet uses two dialects in his epic and mythic

compositions; the main dialect, and another known as the Emesal dialect.

The latter resembles the main dialect very closely and differs only in

showing several regular and characteristic phonetic variations. What is

more interesting, however, is the fact that the poet uses this Emesal

dialect in rendering the direct speech of a female, not male, deity; thus,

the speeches of Inanna, queen of heaven, are regularly rendered in the

Emesal dialect. And so, on examining carefully the texts before me, I realized that what in the case of several passages had been taken to

be a mere meaningless and unmotivated duplication, actually contained a

speech of the goddess Inanna in which she repeats in the Emesal dialect

all that the poet had previously described in narrative form in the main

dialect."

So, in Kramer's findings, a divine message was both given and received; thus, the double recording of the stanza line. In this book, excerpts from the Epic of Gilgamesh are shown only once, although in the Epic they are shown twice, redundantly, as Kramer stated. The use of dual, 'conversational,' dialects is just one example of a hidden plot device in the Epic.

In his book *Gilgamesh among Us*, Theodore Ziokowski suggests that the ancient Sumerian poet was indeed writing an allegory for humankind, while mixing historical records into the plot. This view was influenced by psychologist Carl Jung and the German poet, Rainer Maria Rilke, who wrote, '**Gilgamesh is tremendous**!' We can agree that Gilgamesh is tremendous, mainly because of the many hidden spiritual underpinnings, seemingly encrypted by the brilliant Sumerian poet.

The New Muse Suggested Reading List

A Suggested Reading List

(For those who would "know yet more")

Like many others, this author, a former technocrat, researches via the internet for both well-known and esoteric information. The diligent reader and researcher can find much of the material contained in the *New Muse Book Series* via a series of well-planned, heuristic internet searches. During the creation of the *New Muse Book Series*, the following books were researched or referenced by the author.

A Concise Dictionary of Akkadian', by Black, George and Postgate,

A History of Psychiatry, Ed Shorter

A History of Western Philosophy, Bertrand Russell

A New Earth: Awakening to Your Life's Purpose, Eckhart Tolle

A Simple Path, The Dalai Lama

A Stroke of Insight, Jill Bolte Taylor

A Theory of Everything, Ken Wilbur

A Traveler's Guide for the Afterlife, Mark Mirabello

Ageless Mind, Ageless Body, Deepak Chopra

All you Need Is Love, Jewelle St. James

Alphabet and the Goddess, Leonard Shlain

Ancient Egypt: The Light of the World, Gerald Massey

Ancient Egyptian Symbols: 50 New Discoveries, Meader & Demeter

Ancient History, Israel Smith Clare

As a Man Thinketh, James Allen

Aspects of Christian Mysticism, William Major Scott

Atlantis and the Kingdom of the Neanderthals; 100,000 Years of lost History, Colin Wilson

Autobiography of a Yogi, Paramhansa Yogananda

Autobiography of Wolfgang von Goethe

Barbelo: The Story of Jesus Christ

Beelzebub's Tales to His Grandson, George Gurdjieff

Beyond Belief: The Gospel of Thomas, Elaine Pagels

Beyond the Robot, Gary Lachman

Beyond Theology, Alan Watts

Bhagavad Gita-As It Is, A. C. Bhakti Vedanta Swami Prabhuppada

BioCentrism, Robert Lanza

Biotechnology Unzipped: Promises and Reality, Eric S. Grace

Black Elk Speaks, John Neirhardt

Brave New World, Aldous Huxley

Broca's Brain, Carl Sagan

Buddha and the Gospel of Buddhism, Ananda Kentish Coomaraswamy

Captain of my Ship: Master of my Soul, P. H. Atwater

Care of the Soul, Thomas Moore

Carl Sagan, William Poundstone

Chaos, Gaia, Eros, Ralph Abraham

Chaos, James Gleick

Christian Monasticism, David Knowles

Christian Mysticism, William Ralph Inge

Chuang Tzu: Basic Writings, Burton Watson

Cognizant Mind, Arnold Trehub

Conscious Acts of Creation; The Emergence of a New Physics, Tiller, Dibble, Kohana

Consilience: The Unity of Knowledge, Edward O. Wilson

Contact, Carl Sagan

Cosmos, Carl Sagan

Creative Evolution, Henri Bergson

Croiset: The Clairvoyant, Jack Harrison Pollack

Dancing Wu Li Masters: Seat of Soul, Gary Zarkoff

Dying to Wake Up, Rajiv Parti

Easy Journey to Other Planets, A.C. Bhaktivedanta Swami Prabhupada

Ecstasy: A Study of Secular and Religious Experiences, Marghanita Laski

Embryos, Galaxies, and Sentient Beings: How the Universe Makes Life, Richard Grossinger.

Entangled Minds, Dean Radin

Essential Philosophy, James Mannion

Evolution Isn't What It Used to Be, Walter Truett Anderson.

Extrasensory Perception: Support, Skepticism, and Science, Vol I, II, Edwin May, Sonali Bhatt Marwaha

Filters and Reflections, Jones, Dunne, Jahn

Fire in the Mind: A Biography of Joseph Campbell, Stephan and Robin Larsen

First Steps in Egyptian, Sir Wallis Budge

Freudian Psychology, Calvin S. Hall

Future Shock, Alvin Toffler

Gandhi: An Autobiography

Ghost in the Machine, Arthur Koestler

Guns, Germs, Steel, Jared Diamond

Healing Ancestral Karma, Steven Farmer

Hello from Heaven, Bill and Judy Guggenheim

How Can One Sell the Air? Chief Seattle

Iamblichus' Life of Pythagoras, Thomas Taylor

In Search of the Miraculous, P. D. Ouspensky

Induced After-Death Communication: A Miraculous Therapy for Grief and Loss, Alan L. Botkin, Craig Hogan

Journeys Out of the Body, Robert A. Monroe

Jung, Diedre Bair

Land of the Fallen Star Gods, J. S. Gordon

Leaves of Grass, Walt Whitman

Life after Life, Raymond A. Moody Jr., M.D.

Light on the Yoga Sutras of Patanjali, B. K. S. Iyengar

Living Buddha, Living Christ, Thich Nhat Hanh

Living Conciousness, Metaphysical Vision of Henri Bergson, Barnard

Loitering at the Gate to Eternity: Memoirs of a Psychic Bystander, Louisa Green

Man and His Symbols, Carl G. Jung

Margins of Reality, Robert Jahn, Brenda Dunne

Matter and Mermory, Henri Bergson

Meditations, Marcus Aurelius

Memories, Dreams, and Reflections, Carl G. Jung

Metaphysical Meditations, Paramhansa Yogananda

Milarepa: A Biography, edited by W. Y. Evans-Wentz

Mind to Mind, Rene Warcollier

Mirrors of the Soul, Kahlil Gibran

Modern Philosophy, Roger Scruton

My Religion, Helen Keller

Mysticism and the New Physics, Michael Talbot

Mysticism, Evelyn Underhill

Myths of the Hindus and Buddhists, Ananda Kentish Coomaraswamy,
Sister Nivedita

Names of God, Nathan Stone

No One Here Gets Out Alive: a Biography of Jim Morrison, Jerry Hopkins
and Danny Sugarman

On Death and Dying, Elizabeth Kubler-Ross

Our Roots in the Great Pyramid, Mostafa Elshamy

Peak Experiences, Abraham Maslow

Philosophical Writings, Rene Descartes

Plants of the Gods~ Their Sacred, Healing and Hallucinogenic Powers,
Schultes, Hofmann and Ratsch

Popal Vuh, Dennis Tedlock

Powers of Mind, Adam Smith

Psychic Discoveries Behind the Iron Curtain, Ostrander and Schroeder

Psycho-Cybernetics, Maxwell Maltz

Quantum Healing, Deepak Chopra

Raising the Earth to the Next Vibration, Richard Grossinger

A Brief History of Time, Stephen Hawking

A History of God, Karen Armstrong

Reflections on Life after Life, Raymond A. Moody Jr., MD

Remote Viewers; The Secret History of America's Psychic Spies, Jim Schnabel

Remote Viewing Secrets, Joseph McMoneagle

Science and the Akashic Field, Ervin Laszlo

Science Set Free, Rupert Sheldrake

Selected Poems: Keats, Edited by George H. Ford

Serpent in the Sky: High Wisdom of Ancient Egypt, John Anthony West

Serpent in the Sky; The Ancient Wisdom of Ancient Egypt, Jonathan Anthony West

Seth Speaks, Jane Roberts

Stalking the Wild Pendulum: On the Mechanics of Consciousness, Itzhak Bentov

Still Here, Ram Dass

Surely, You're Joking, Mr. Feldman, Richard Feldman

Tales of Wonder, Huston Smith

Tao Te Ching, Lao-Tzu, Gia-Fu-Feng, Jane English

Teachings of Sufism, Carl W. Ernst

Tertium Organum, P. D. Ouspensky

The Afterlife of Billy Fingers, Annie Kagan

The Akashic Experience: Science and the Cosmic Memory Field, Ervin Lazslo

The Ancient History of Egyptians, Assyrians, Vol. 1 & 2, Charles Rollin

The Ancient Wisdom, Annie Besant

The Art of Thinking Clearly, Rolf Dobelli

The Autobiography of Mark Twain

The Autobiography of Rudolph Steiner

The Bicameral Critic, Colin Wilson

The Biology of Transcendence, Joseph Chilton Pearce

The Black Swan, Nissan Nicholas Taleb

The Body Electric, Bob Becker

The Body of Myth, J. Nigro Sansonese

The Book Your Church Doesn't Want You to Read, Tim Leedom

The Christian Conspiracy, Dr. David Moore

The Closing of the American Mind, Allen Bloom

The Collected Wisdom of Heraclitus, Brooks Haxton

The Coming Era in Science: New York Times, Edited by Holcomb B. Noble

The Complete Illuminated Books of William Blake

The Complete Works of Count Tolstoy: Walk in the Light While Ye Have Light

The Complete Works of Swami Vivekananda

The Conscious Universe, Dean Radin.

The Crack in the Cosmic Egg; Challenging Constructs of Mind and Reality, Joseph Chilton Pearce

The Crown of Life: A Study in Yoga, Kirpal Singh

The Dance of Siva, Ananda Kentish Coomaraswamy

The Dancing Wu Li Masters, Gary Zukav

The Dead Sea Scrolls Uncovered, R. Eisenmann, M. Wise

The Dialogues of Plato, Erich Segal

The Divided Brain and the Search for Meaning: Why Are We So Unhappy? Iain McGilChrist

The Doors of Perception, Aldous Huxley

The Dragons of Eden, Carl Sagan

The Dream Culture of the Neanderthals, Stan Gooch

The Egyptian Book of the Dead (and Great Awakening), Dr. Muata Ashby

The Egyptian Book of the Dead (and Great Awakening), Sir Wallis E. Budge

The Elegant Universe, Brian Greene

The End of Faith, Sam Harris

The End of Suffering and the Discovery of Happiness: The Path of Tibetan Buddhism, The Dalai Lama

The Essential Blake, Stanley Kunitz

The Essential Jesus, John Dominic Crossan

The Field, Lynn Taggart

The Flight of the Eagle, J. Krishnamurti

The Four Agreements Companion Book, Don Miguel Ruiz

The Future of the Mind, Michio Kaku

The Future, Al Gore

The God Delusion, Richard Dawkins

The Gospel According to Jesus, Stephen Mitchell

The Gospel According to Zen: Beyond the Death of God, Robert Sohl and Audrey Carr

The Gospel of Sri Rama Krishna, Vivekananda Center

The Great Chain of Being, Arthur Lovejoy

The Hand, Frank R. Wilson

The Heart's Code, Paul Pearsall

The HeartMath Solution, Childre & Martin

The Heart-Mind Matrix, Joseph Chilton Pierce

The Heaven at the End of Science, Philip Mereton

The Hero with a Thousand Faces, Joseph Campbell

The Hidden Jesus, Donald Spoto

The Holographic Universe, Michael Talbot

The Illuminated Rumi, Coleman Barks

The Inner Treasure: An Introduction to the World's Sacred and Mystical Writings, Jonathan Star

The Intention Experiment, Lynn Talbert.

The Invisible Gorilla, Cristopher Chabris, Daniel Simons.

The Joseph Campbell Phenomenon, Lawrence Madden

The Joyous Cosmology, Alan W. Watts

The King James Version of the Holy Bible

The Lady Tasting Tea: How Statistics Revolutionized Science in the 20th Century, David Salsburg

The Life of Sir Isaac Newton, Sir David Brewster

The Living Thoughts of Gotama, Ananda Kentish Coomaraswamy

The Lost Years of Jesus Revealed, Rev. Dr. Francis Potter

The Lost Years of Jesus, Elizabeth Clare Prophet

The Marriage of Heaven and Hell, Aldous Huxley

The Masks of God: Creative Mythology, Joseph Campbell

The Masks of God: Occidental Mythology, Joseph Campbell

The Masks of God: Oriental Mythology, Joseph Campbell

The Masks of God: Primitive Mythology, Joseph Campbell

The Master and His Emissary: The Divided Brain and the Making of the Western World, Iain McGilChrist

The Mind-Boggling Universe, James McAleer

The Mystical Mind: Probing the Biology of Religious Experience, D'Aquili, Newburg

The Myth of the Eternal Return, Mircea Eliade

The Myth of the Machine: The Pentagon of Power, Lewis Mumford

The Mythic Image, Joseph Campbell.

The Notebooks of Leonardo da Vinci, Edward MacKurdy

The Origin of Consciousness and the Breakdown of the Bi-Cameral Mind, Julian Jaynes

The Origin of Species, Charles Darwin

The Other Bible, editor William Barnstone

The Outline of History, H. G. Wells

The Pentagon of Power, Lewis Mumford

The Philosophies of India, Heinrich Zimmer

The Portable Jung, edited by Joseph Campbell

The Power of Now, Eckhart Tolle

The Primeval Flood Catastrophe: Origins and Early Development in Mesopotamian Traditions (Oxford Oriental Monographs) by Y. S. Chen

The Prema-Sagara (Ocean of Love), Kavi Lal

The Presence of the Past: Morphic Resonance and the Habits of Nature, Rupert Sheldrake

The Psychology of Transcendence, Andrew Neher

The Quotable Einstein, Alice Calaprice

The Republic, Plato, translated by Benjamin Jowett

The Rosetta Stone, Sir Wallis Budge

The Scalpel and the Soul: Encounters with Surgery, Allan J. Hamilton

The Search for Bridey Murphy, Morey Bernstine

The Search for Omm Sety, Jonathan Cott

The Secret Path, Paul Brunton

The Secret Teachers of the Western World, Gary Lachman

The Selfish Gene, Richard Dawkins

The Singing Neanderthal, Steven Mithen

The Song of God: Bhagavad Gita, Christopher Isherwood, Swami Prabhavananda

The Supreme Adventure, Robert Crooke

The Tao of Physics, F. Capra

The Teachings of Don Juan: A Yaqui Way of Knowledge, Carlos Castaneda

The Teachings of Rumi, Andrew Harvey

The Tibetan Book of the Dead (Great Liberation), W. Y. Evans-Wentz

The Travelers Key to Ancient Egypt, John Anthony West

The Universe in a Single Atom: The Convergence of Science and Spirituality, The Dalai Lama

The Universe Within: The History of the Human Body, Neil Shubin

The Untethered Soul, Michael Singer

The Upanishads, Sri Aurobindo

The Vanishing Peoples of the Earth, National Geographic Society

The Varieties of Religious Experience, William James

The Wanderer, Kahlil Gibran

The World of the Druids, Miranda J. Green.

Think on These Things, J. Krishnamurti

Through My Eyes, Gordon Smith

Thus Spoke Zarathustra, Friedrich Nietzsche

Unconditional Life, Deepak Chopra

Varieties of Anomalous Experience, Cardena, Lynn, Krippener

Vistas of Infinity, Jurgen Ziewe

Waking Up in Time: Finding Inner Peace in Times of Accelerating Change, Peter Russell

Why God Won't Go Away: Brain Science and the Biology of Belief, Newberg; Andrew; D'Aquili; Eugene

Why Socrates Died, Robin WaterField

Your Eternal Self, Craig Hogan

Index

About the Author

A High-Low Bio

Steven A. Key, in a former technological life, had a career taming the largest computer systems in the world—those rascally mainframes folks often hear about. As a deep-researching computerist and technocrat, he was readily primed to combine his investigative skills with his deep personal interests in all things pertaining to body, mind and spirit. Combining unique approaches to neuroscience, psychology, consciousness, and ancient history, Steven created the *New Muse Book Series*. His initial book, *The Secret Yoga of the Vikings*, is the first book of its kind in that it reveals the hidden Yoga of the tenth-century Norse poets. This secret has been extremely well kept and is now revealed anew for the first time in over a thousand years, via the skeleton key of Raja Yoga.

~

The above loosely assembled biographical information gives the public and the publisher sufficient insight to establish an author's persona but, on the other hand, defeats the entire purpose of the author's writings concerning consciousness and neuropsychology as Yoga.

The real biographical information of people should include a description of their deepest nature and selves. Socrates referred to his deeper nature as his spiritually guiding Daimon. Siddartha mystically informed his disciples to be "intimate with the Lovely" as a guiding lamp. We are the House of the Holy. It's important to put that in the bio; otherwise, it's simply an egotistical expression of personality.

Another aspect of a high-low bio involves an appreciative association with one's parents, as the Upanishads state. Thus, in the light of Yoga, one's mother and father are seen as God-like beings—Goddess and God—for the fantastic provisions, whether good or bad, that they provide to the child—their living, breathing representative of themselves. It's good to be an apple from that tree. A high-low bio should include the entirety of humanity, as sisters and brothers, for we are all gifted in the same neurological fashion, in having a lower and a higher nature. We then extend, sentiently, into the universe for all creatures large or small. We are all of the same root. As for springing from my karma and its reincarnation via my parents, it's essential to point out that, generally, people have only a single-life view; that of their Ego. This is what the Greeks called anamnesis—the great forgetting. As one forgets at birth, the Ego grows and believes its life to be the sole reality. As one proceeds along the path of life that all humans must journey, additional glimpses and insightful experiences of past lives can result in one's accepting a multi-life view, which this author endorses as another deep, essential facet in this high-low bio.

"You know how little while we have to stay.

The Way You go up is the Way You came Down.

The Labyrinth… is in You Now."

Steven A. Key

Made in the USA
Middletown, DE
24 August 2020

16692734R00097